OSPREY COMBAT AIRCRAFT 106

SAVOIA-MARCHETTI S.79 *SPARVIERO* TORPEDO-BOMBER UNITS

SERIES EDITOR TONY HOLMES

OSPREY COMBAT AIRCRAFT 106

SAVOIA-MARCHETTI S.79 *SPARVIERO* TORPEDO-BOMBER UNITS

MARCO MATTIOLI

OSPREY
PUBLISHING

Front Cover
During World War 2 it was customary in the *Regia Aeronautica* for the individual numeral '1' on a fuselage to indicate a unit leader's aircraft. Of course there were exceptions to this rule, and *Sparviero* MM23973, coded 280-6, was one such machine. This trimotor was often flown by Capitano Franco Melley, CO of 130° *Gruppo Autonomo AS*. On 22 March 1942 it was Melley's mount during the Second Battle of Sirte, and he was also at the aircraft's controls during the 18 May 1942 dusk attack on the carrier HMS *Argus* southwest of Sardinia and when the cruiser HMS *Cairo* and its four escort destroyers were targeted on 17 June 1942.

During the hard-fought *Pedestal* battle on 12 August 1942, 280-6 was flown by Capitano Angelo Caponetti. Although the aircraft sustained damage from fighter attacks during this action, its gunners in turn claimed a Sea Hurricane shot down and another 'probable'.

On 10 November 1942 280-6 temporarily passed to Maggiore Massimiliano Erasi for the action that saw 130° *Gruppo Sparvieri* sink the British sloop HMS *Ibis* north of Algiers. Two days later the aircraft was again in Capitano Melley's hands when he flew it in a dramatic afternoon sortie over Bougie Bay that resulted in the loss of Sottotenente Nino Meschiari and *Sparviero* 280-2 to deadly anti-aircraft fire. On 2 December 1942 280-6's starboard engine failed and Melley was forced to turn back to base, thus escaping the dramatic *Sparvieri* massacre by No 242 Sqn Spitfires later that day.

In this specially commissioned cover artwork, artist Mark Postlethwaite has portrayed *Sparviero* 280-6 of Capitano Franco Melley during the 17 June 1942 torpedo attack on the cruiser *Cairo* 20 miles northwest of Galite island

Dedication
To my dear nephew Paolo, 'our little sun', and to his parents, Gianni and Nicoletta. To my father, Fabrizio, and my mother Flory. To Generale Giulio Cesare Graziani, torpedo-bomber ace, who honoured me with his praise.

First published in Great Britain in 2014 by Osprey Publishing
PO Box 883, Oxford, OX1 9PL, UK
PO Box 3985, New York, NY 10185-3985, USA

E-mail: info@ospreypublishing.com

Osprey Publishing is part of the Osprey Group

A CIP catalogue record for this book is available from the British Library

ISBN: 978 1 78200 807 1
PDF e-book ISBN: 978 1 78200 808 8
e-Pub ISBN: 978 1 78200 809 5

Edited by Tony Holmes and Philip Jarrett
Cover Artwork by Mark Postlethwaite
Aircraft Profiles by Richard Caruana
Index by Fionbar Lyons
Originated by PDQ Digital Media Solutions, UK
Printed in China through Asia Pacific Offset Limited

14 15 16 17 18   10 9 8 7 6 5 4 3 2 1

Osprey Publishing is supporting the Woodland Trust, the UK's leading woodland conservation charity, by funding the dedication of trees.

www.ospreypublishing.com

Acknowledgements
The author would like to thank his friends Maurizio Di Terlizzi, Gianni Panebianco, the late Nino Arena, Andrea Marescalchi and both military and civilian personnel of the Italian Air Force and Italian Army Historical Services for their help with the compilation of this book.

CONTENTS

INTRODUCTION 6

CHAPTER ONE
1940 – THE BEGINNING 7

CHAPTER TWO
1941 – TORPEDO-BOMBERS COME OF AGE 13

CHAPTER THREE
1942 – A YEAR OF BATTLES 29

CHAPTER FOUR
1943 – YEAR OF DESTINY 67

CHAPTER FIVE
***SPARVIERI* TO THE NORTH 80**

APPENDICES 88
COLOUR PLATES COMMENTARY 91
INDEX 96

INTRODUCTION

On 13 November 1942 *War Bulletin* No 901 informed an astonished Italian people that one of the *Regia Aeronautica*'s (Italian Air Force's) most famous heroes, Maggiore Carlo Emanuele Buscaglia, a torpedo-bomber ace, was missing in action following an attack on Bougie Harbour in Algeria. This *Osprey Combat Aircraft* volume spotlights Buscaglia and his fellow airmen who flew the *Regia Aeronautica*'s torpedo-bombers, which were among the most lethal weapons fielded by Italy during the Mediterranean war.

The Italians, notably lawyer Raoul Pateras-Pescara and Captain of Naval Engineering Alessandro Guidoni, had conducted tests of aerial torpedoes from 1914. Some aerial torpedo attacks had been attempted as early as World War 1, but to no avail. Trials continued through the 1920s and 1930s using several aircraft types, until in 1938 the first aerial torpedo produced by the Whitehead firm of Fiume was paired with the SIAI Marchetti (also known as Savoia-Marchetti) S.79, later named *Sparviero* (Sparrowhawk). Thanks to its remarkable speed and manoeuvrability, the S.79 was destined to become the Italian aircraft of choice for the torpedo-bomber role.

Yet, owing to rivalries between the Italian Navy and Air Force, which disputed each other's control and financing of the new role, Italy entered the war in 1940 lacking trained crews, specialised units and sufficient air-launched torpedoes to wage an adequate anti-shipping war. This situation was aggravated by the poor performance of the Italian level bombers, whose weapons, dropped from too high an altitude, dispersed and mostly failed to hit enemy ships. Those aboard the targeted vessels were usually able to spot and avoid the falling bombs, although the ships were often straddled and, in many cases, suffered damage from near misses.

Luckily, *Generale di Squadra Aerea* Francesco Pricolo, the *Regia* Aeronautica's Chief of Staff since November 1939, intervened to resolve this absurd situation. Pricolo was a strong supporter of the potential new torpedo-bomber branch, and shortly after his appointment he had hastily ordered a batch of 30 aerial torpedoes from Whitehead. To further accelerate this process following Italy's entry into the war, Pricolo ordered a further batch of 50 aerial torpedoes (formerly allocated to Germany) for the air force's new role in July 1940. Thanks to his initiative, Italy at least had a modest quantity of torpedoes at its disposal during the first months of war. Otherwise, there would have been nothing.

In the torpedo-bomber role the S.79 proved to be an insuperable and outstanding aircraft. Thanks to the heroism of their crews, the *Sparvieri* sank and damaged a number of Allied ships and became a constant threat to Allied naval convoys in the Mediterranean. The successes they achieved, in spite of suffering heavy losses, earned the torpedo-armed S.79 the nickname *Gobbi Maledetti* (damned hunchbacks) due to the distinctive dorsal hump of the aircraft's cockpit roof. The S.79 was permanently associated with the most skilled torpedo aces, celebrated in wartime Italy as true heroes just as fighter aces were in other belligerent countries.

With these airmen aboard, the deeds of the *Sparvieri* became almost legendary, making the aircraft as famous to the Italians as Mustangs, Spitfires and Messerschmitts were to the Americans, British and Germans, respectively. Due to their achievements, which made them the *Regia* Aeronautica's most lethal wartime weapon, the S.79s were considered extremely successful. Indeed, they were worthy of being counted among the most effective land-based torpedo-bombers of the whole conflict.

1940 – THE BEGINNING

As already related, following the disappointing performance of Italian high-level bombers in the anti-shipping war, Generale Pricolo urgently ordered that the first Italian torpedo-bomber unit be rushed into action. Thus on 25 July 1940 at Gorizia-Merna airfield, the so-called *Reparto Sperimentale Aerosiluranti* (Experimental Torpedo-bomber Unit, later renamed *'Speciale'*) was officially formed.

The first CO of the new unit was Capitano Amedeo Mojoli, who, some days later, handed over command to Maggiore Vincenzo Dequal. Five handpicked pilots and crews had been assigned to the unit. The pilots were Maggiore Enrico Fusco, Tenenti Carlo Emanuele Buscaglia, Franco Melley and Carlo Copello and Sottotenente Guido Robone. Naval officers Tenente di Vascello Giovanni Marazio and Sottotenente di Vascello Giovanni Bertoli were also assigned to the unit as underwater weapons specialists.

Between 23 July and 5 August the unit took on charge seven S.79s fitted with torpedo crutches. After undertaking a hasty training period, the *Aerosiluranti* were ready to make their operational debut. The *Regia Aeronautica* thus acquired a new type of unit, whose S.79s left Gorizia on 10 August 1940 for North Africa. The next day the aircraft stopped over at Rome-Ciampino airport so that the pilots could meet Generale Pricolo in the Italian capital. With the formalities over, the unit set off for Libya, the S.79s reaching Tobruk T5 airfield on the 12th and subsequently moving to El Adem airfield, which was deemed to be more suitable for torpedo-bomber operations.

The first targets for the *Aerosiluranti*'s combat debut were Royal Navy warships anchored in Alexandria harbour. On 15 August 1940 the five *Reparto Speciale Aerosiluranti* S.79s, flown by Maggiori Dequal and Fusco, Tenenti Buscaglia, Copello and Melley and Sottotenente Robone and their crews, took off from El Adem at 1928 hrs. Each aircraft carried one 450 mm Whitehead torpedo slung in the port ventral position. These weapons were 5.46 m (17.9 ft) long, weighed about 876 kg (1930 lb) and had an explosive charge of 170 kg (374.5 lb). The feasibility of carrying two torpedoes had been tested, but this seriously impaired the S.79's performance. Hampered by mist and low clouds, the aircraft reached their objective between 2130 hrs and 2145 hrs. Splitting into two formations, they were 'welcomed' by fierce anti-aircraft fire.

Three S.79s were forced to abandon the mission because of poor visibility over the target and dangerous fuel shortages. The action was vividly described by 1° Aviere Marconista Giuseppe Dondi, a wireless operator aboard Tenente Copello's aircraft;

Maggiore Vincenzo Dequal replaced Capitano Amedeo Mojoli as CO of the *Reparto Sperimentale Aerosiluranti* in the summer of 1940 (*Aeronautica Militare*)

'Six hundred, five hundred, four hundred metres and these damned clouds are even lower – here is the trick! At last we emerge at less than 100 metres, and straight as a spindle we find ourselves over a deserted enemy beach. One tight turn to the left brings us over open sea again. Alexandria cannot be far. These damned clouds want to trick us. We head in again, and as if by magic one, two, ten, thirty searchlights switch on, their beams combing the sky, crossing one another, pursuing us, lifting and lowering in a possessed dance.

'We are again immersed in cloud, and find ourselves in a hellish pit that even Dante [Dante Alighieri, the famous medieval Italian poet who envisioned a journey to hell in his *Divine Comedy* – author] could not have remotely imagined. The fireworks of Venice and Naples are nothing by comparison. Intersecting tracers rocket into the sky, forming the most beautiful hieroglyphics that one could imagine. They are white, red, blue – all colours. They whistle, as if to give us our first greeting. Much higher up, strange flashes switch on and off. The anti-aircraft artillery is welcoming us.

'We are perfectly in the harbour's centre, at wavetop level, but the drop is impossible. The white houses of Alexandria stand out neatly in the darkness, and the pier as a long arm stretches out into the sea, almost as if it were enfolding the vast number of ships in the harbour in a protective embrace. Beyond the harbour there is a second circular basin, and on the strip of land dividing the two harbours the batteries are doing their duty, illuminating the water with their sinister flashes. We nose up, make a perfect turnabout, and again find ourselves out of range. The searchlights continue their futile efforts. It is useless trying again – instead, we will begin the return flight home, and the drama.'

An S.79 loaded with two torpedoes. This option was trialled but rejected when it was realised that such a heavy load badly affected the S.79's performance. From then on the only time aircraft were seen with two torpedoes underslung was during transport flights

Tenenti Guido Robone, Carlo Emanuele Buscaglia and Carlo Copello were among the first pilots to pioneer torpedo-bomber techniques both in the *Reparto Speciale Aerosiluranti* and 278ª *Squadriglia AS* (*via author*)

A torpedo-laden *Sparviero* (individually coded 4) photographed from below. S.79s of the *Aerosiluranti* were typically armed with a single 876 kg Whitehead torpedo (*Aeronautica Militare*)

Capitano Massimiliano Erasi replaced Maggiore Dequal at the head of 278ª *Squadriglia Aut AS* in September 1940. With its new CO, the unit inflicted heavy damage on the cruisers HMS *Kent*, HMS *Liverpool* and HMS *Glasgow*, the last two falling victim to Erasi himself. He subsequently served as CO of 284ª *Squadriglia* and 41° *Gruppo*, instructed with 1° *Nucleo AS* and flew with 130° *Gruppo AS* (*Aeronautica Militare*)

The aircraft of Robone and Copello had to force-land in Italian-held territory, but they were able to return to base after being refuelled. Fusco's S.79 landed behind enemy lines, he and his crew being captured after having set their S.79 alight to prevent it from falling into British hands. However, the other two S.79s, flown by Maggiore Dequal (S.79 '6') and Tenente Buscaglia (S.79 '2') dropped their torpedoes, aiming at the cruiser HMS *Gloucester*. Unfortunately the weapons sank in the harbour's mudbanks and the ship escaped unscathed. Despite heavy anti-aircraft fire Dequal and Buscaglia managed to disengage.

Although it was unsuccessful, this attack marked the S.79's debut as a torpedo-bomber in the war. The loss of Fusco and his crew left the unit with just four aircrews, and it henceforth became known as the *'Quattro Gatti'* ('Four Cats', Italian slang for very few people). At the time few realised that this nickname would become legendary.

278ª *SQUADRIGLIA'S* FIRST SUCCESSES

The 'Four Cats' tried to attack Alexandria again on 23 August, with Robone and, on the 27th, Buscaglia carrying out the first attack on ships in open sea. Both actions proved ineffective.

On 3 September the *Reparto Speciale Aerosiluranti* was re-titled the 278ª *Squadriglia Autonoma Aerosiluranti*. The unit's emblem was four cats (two black and two white) and its motto was *Pauci sed semper immites* (Few, but always aggressive). Tradition has it that the 'Four Cats' insignia was the idea of Capitano Massimiliano Erasi, the unit's new CO, who had taken over from Maggiore Dequal, and that it was drawn by aeronautical engineer Sottotenente Alessandro Maffei. Under its new CO the unit soon achieved its first real successes.

The torpedo S.79s scored their first confirmed hit on 17 September when the cruiser HMS *Kent* was ordered to shell Bardia along with the destroyers HMS *Mohawk* and HMS *Nubian*. At 2240 hrs, before the bombardment could begin, the cruiser was attacked by two S.79 torpedo-bombers flown by Tenenti Robone (in 278-1) and Buscaglia (278-2). The Italians attacked with the moonlight in their favour, the moon being about 90 degrees to starboard, which allowed the pilots to see *Kent* from a distance of 700 m. The two S.79s dropped both of their torpedoes and one struck *Kent*, damaging it badly. The 9850-ton cruiser was hit aft, near the propeller shafts on its starboard side, resulting in a significant loss of life. Two officers and 31 ratings were killed, and the ship remained stationary in the water, its anti-aircraft fire stopping at once. Although the S.79s had taken some ack-ack hits, they made for their base at El Adem, where they landed safely at 2330 hrs.

Sub Lt George Blundell, an officer aboard the crippled cruiser, later recalled Kent's torpedoing;

'We were then firing hard at aircraft, and I remember distinctly thinking that we'd got a direct hit on one, but it may have been only a shell bursting. Then we had a low torpedo-bomber attack on our starboard beam. I saw the splashes, enormous ones, as the torpedoes were dropped. Shortly afterwards there was a tremendous blow aft.

'The whole ship reeled, then suddenly went dead, and we could feel on the bridge as if her tail had dropped – a sort of bending, dragging feeling. The ship wouldn't steer. We were then machine-gunned by aircraft that came in from ahead. I didn't realise what it was at first, except that there were loud cracks, just like one hears when standing in rifle butts, whilst red worms seemed to fly all around us. At first I thought they were sparks from the funnel. It was too fascinating to be in the least frightening, but when I realised they were bullets I knelt down to present a smaller target.'

S.79 278-1, seen here in the autumn of 1940, was often flown by Tenente Guido Robone. On 3 September that year the *Reparto Speciale Aerosiluranti* was redesignated 278ª *Squadriglia Autonoma Aerosiluranti* (*Aeronautica Militare*)

Badly damaged, *Kent* was towed with great difficulty to Alexandria by the destroyer *Nubian*, screened by the cruiser HMS *Orion* and the anti-aircraft ship HMS *Calcutta*, along with the destroyers HMS *Jervis*, HMS *Janus*, HMS *Juno*, HMS *Mohawk* and HMAS *Vendetta*. The vessel reached the naval base safely on 19 September, its dead being buried at sea from the netlayer HMS *Protector* that same evening. The attack put the cruiser out of commission for a year, repairs being completed in Great Britain on 20 September 1941.

From 19 September 1940 the Italian *Superaereo* High Command, aiming to stir the Italian people's interest in Italy's air war and seeking better identification of the force's aircraft, decided that each aircraft type should have a name. Thenceforth the S.79s were officially known as *Sparvieri*, a name destined to become famous.

Less than a month after torpedoing *Kent*, 278ª *Squadriglia* gained its second victory. At 1855 hrs on 14 October 1940, the cruiser HMS *Liverpool*, after escorting a Malta-bound convoy in Operation MB 6, was torpedoed by S.79 278-6, piloted by Capitano Massimiliano Erasi. The attack took place in the Aegean Sea, 60 miles south of Cape Misi (Crete's eastern tip). Erasi headed towards the moon and, flying under a layer of cloud, spotted the British cruiser almost immediately below him. *Liverpool*'s captain took evasive action, forcing Erasi to make three attack runs, but he was able to drop his torpedo on the third pass. After a fire started in *Liverpool*, an explosion in its petrol and ammunition holds wrecked the bow just ahead of the bridge. Three officers and 24 ratings were lost, and three more ratings died of wounds. Forty-two ratings were wounded.

While the anti-aircraft cruiser *Calcutta* again provided a screen, *Liverpool* was taken in tow aft by the cruiser *Orion*, which dragged the ship laboriously for 100 miles at a speed of nine knots. Speed was increased after the broken bow detached, allowing both ships to enter Alexandria at midnight on the 16th. *Liverpool* remained out of commission for more than a year.

On 7 November Maggiore Dequal, Tenenti Buscaglia, Melley, Robone, Copello and Galimberti and other NCO pilots of 278ᵃ *Squadriglia* were decorated with the *Medaglia d'Argento al Valor Militare* (Silver Medal for Military Valour) by Generale Felice Porro, 5ᵃ *Squadra Aerea* AOC. Several of the unit's specialist under-officers and airmen (including airman Dondi) were also awarded the Bronze Medal for Military Valour.

278ᵃ *Squadriglia*'s third confirmed success was scored on 3 December 1940. On that day two of the unit's S.79s, 278-6 and 278-2, flown by Capitano Massimiliano Erasi and Tenente Carlo Emanuele Buscaglia, respectively, took off from El Adem at 1315 hrs. By 1536 hrs the two torpedo-bombers were over Crete and, passing over the mountain range in the southwest of the island, they headed north, diving steeply through the overcast that entirely covered the island at 1000 m (3300 ft). Emerging from the clouds, the Italians suddenly sighted Souda Bay, and at once began their attack approach, initially overflying the road from Armeni to Hania.

At 1550 hrs the two S.79s began the final attack run, targeting the two cruisers HMS *Glasgow* and HMS *Gloucester*, anchored in the bay. They were protected by an anti-torpedo net barrage 300 m (330 yds) away from them, with a 20-degree orientation. Adm Andrew Cunningham, Commander-in-Chief, Mediterranean, later stated that *Glasgow* was hit by 'two aircraft approaching from the entrance of the bay'. Almost at once the ships opened up with a fierce defence, but the two S.79s dropped their torpedoes at 700 m (770 yds) range at an angle of 100 degrees, trying to avoid the net barrage.

The light cruiser *Glasgow* was hit by two torpedoes on its starboard side and seriously damaged. The first weapon, which struck at 1550 hrs, made a large hole in the starboard side forward and caused structural damage and flooding. The second struck at 1551 hrs and hit the starboard side aft, putting 'X' turret out of service and damaging two propeller shafts. One officer and two ratings were killed and three ratings seriously wounded by the explosions. The two S.79s then headed north, escaping over the Kalepa Peninsula despite fierce anti-aircraft fire. At 1552 hrs they turned 270 degrees, climbing above the clouds that covered the area and heading south for Libya at 1556 hrs.

Two days later *Glasgow* reached Alexandria, sailing at 16 knots and escorted by *Gloucester* and the destroyers HMS *Hereward* and HMS *Hasty*, with the usual protection of the anti-aircraft ship *Calcutta*. *Glasgow* remained out of commission for nine months, leaving Alexandria in February 1941 after temporary repairs had been carried out. It underwent further repairs in the East Indies in the summer of 1941 and was fully overhauled in New York Naval Yard between May and August 1942.

Having enjoyed success against *Glasgow*, Erasi became one of the more prominent torpedo-bomber aces. After the Italian armistice in September 1943 he joined the Italian Co-belligerent Air Force (ICAF), fighting on the Allied side. Erasi was killed in combat on

The badly damaged bow of the cruiser HMS *Liverpool* after Capitano Erasi's successful torpedo attack on 14 October 1940. The British warship was put out of commission for more than a year (*via author*)

21 February 1945 while flying an ICAF Martin Baltimore twin-engined bomber, earning him a posthumous award of the *Medaglia d'Oro al Valor Militare* (Gold Medal for Military Valour).

Altogether, in their first four months of combat in 1940, the *Aerosiluranti* of 278ª *Squadriglia* had dropped 37 torpedoes and hit three British cruisers for the loss of one S.79 (its crew being captured).

Meanwhile, to enhance torpedo-bomber force development, the *Regia Aeronautica* organised training units, named *Nuclei Addestramento Aerosiluranti* (also identified in official documents as *Nuclei Addestramento Siluranti* (*AS*)). On 26 October 1940 1° *Nucleo AS* was formed at Gorizia, followed by 2° *Nucleo AS* on 25 November at Naples-Capodichino airport. Finally, 3° *Nucleo AS* was formed at Pisa-San Giusto airfield on 15 January 1942.

It is worth emphasising that, as reported in its war diary, 2° *Nucleo AS* used the type S I (*Siluro Italiano*) torpedo for training. Built by the Baia torpedo factory in Naples, the 450 mm weapon was employed by Italian torpedo-bombers alongside the Whitehead torpedo. The S I differed from the Whitehead in length, being 5.25 m (17.22 ft) long.

The 1° *Nucleo AS*, led by Tenente Colonnello Carlo Unia, trained 279ª *Squadriglia* AS, which formed on 26 December 1940. 1° *Nucleo* and 2° *Nucleo AS* cooperated to establish a further four S.79-equipped *squadriglie*, namely 280ª (formed on 8 February 1941 and led by Capitano Mojoli), 281ª (formed on 5 March 1941 and led by Capitano Buscaglia), 283ª (formed on 4 July 1941 and led by Capitano Giorgio Grossi) and 284ª (formed on 7 November 1941 and led by Capitano Erasi).

As regards Tenente Colonnello Unia's contribution to the *Aerosiluranti* force, besides being a worthy commanding officer, he also conceived (together with Tenente di Vascello Oss Marazio) a practical torpedo-aiming sight, the *Grafometro* (Graphometer) – the first S.79s had lacked such a device. Once introduced into service the *Grafometro* proved to be particularly useful, for it enabled its operators to aim accurately at their targets. This innovative piece of equipment was subsequently fitted on the instrument panels of all S.79s issued to frontline units from *Nuclei AS*.

Sparviero 280-1 of 280ª *Squadriglia* flies low over the sea off Sardinia. This unit, trained by 1° *Nucleo AS*, was formed on 8 February 1941 and put under Capitano Mojoli's command (*Aeronautica Militare*)

An example of the *Grafometro* ship-aiming gear on an S.79 instrument panel. This useful targeting device, created by Tenente Colonnello Carlo Unia, along with observer Tenente di Vascello Giovanni Marazio, soon began to equip all *Sparvieri* flown by the *Aerosiluranti* (*Aeronautica Militare*)

1941 – TORPEDO-BOMBERS COME OF AGE

On 10 January 1941 at 1223 hrs, southeast of Pantelleria, two S.79s of 279ᵃ *Squadriglia*, flown by Capitano Orazio Bernardini (with Tenente di Vascello Domenico Baffigo aboard as observer) and Tenente Angelo Caponetti, attacked a British naval convoy, including the aircraft carrier HMS *Illustrious*, that was heading for Malta as part of Operation *Excess*. The two S.79s dropped their torpedoes at 2500 m (2730 yds) range, missing the battleship HMS *Valiant* aft.

Both aircraft were then intercepted by four Fairey Fulmar fighters of 806 Naval Air Squadron (NAS), Fleet Air Arm (FAA), which pursued them for 20 miles and badly damaged Tenente Caponetti's S.79 – the crippled torpedo-bomber crashed on landing at Trapani. However, the Savoias had distracted the Fulmars, enabling Sicilian-based Ju 87 Stukas of the Luftwaffe's I./StG 1 and II./StG 2 to score six hits with bombs (and three near misses) on the unfortunate carrier. *Illustrious* was then attacked again at 1610 hrs by Italian Stukas of 96° *Gruppo BaT*, which scored one further bomb hit and two near misses. The carrier was badly damaged, and suffered significant loss of life. After this action, on 27 January, 279ᵃ *Squadriglia* moved to Gerbini, in Sicily.

As already noted, 281ᵃ *Squadriglia* was formed on 5 March 1941 at Grottaglie airport (Apulia) with four S.79s, its CO, Capitano Buscaglia, having previously served with the famous 278ᵃ *Squadriglia*. Deployed to Gadurra (on the island of Rhodes) on 20 March, the new unit included such accomplished pilots as Tenenti Greco, Cimicchi and Sacchetti, who were later joined by others such as Tenenti Graziani, Faggioni, Forzinetti, Rovelli, Cipelletti, Spezzaferri and Fiumani. On Rhodes, 281ᵃ *Squadriglia* operated alongside 34° *Gruppo Autonomo BT*, which also had five S.79 torpedo-bombers assigned to 67ᵃ and 68ᵃ *Squadriglie*.

On the night of 10 March at 2100 hrs, ten Wellington bombers of Nos 37 and 70 Sqns raided Gadurra and Maritza airfields, destroying a 67ᵃ *Squadriglia* S.79 torpedo-bomber at the former location and splinter-damaging two S.79 bombers at the latter airfield.

On 10 January 1941 two S.79s of 279ᵃ *Squadriglia* attacked a British naval convoy southeast of Pantelleria, their torpedoes passing aft of the battleship HMS *Valiant*. Left to right are three protagonists from this action – Tenente Angelo Caponetti, Capitano Orazio Bernardini and naval observer Tenente di Vascello Osservatore Domenico Baffigo (*Italian Army/SME*)

On 21 March two 68ª *Squadriglia* aircraft flown by Maggiore Vittorio Cannaviello and Capitano Giorgio Grossi attacked a British convoy southwest of Cape Krio. Having missed a cruiser the S.79s were bounced by three Fulmars at 1225 hrs, but the FAA fighters were driven off by effective return fire. The following day three S.79 torpedo-bombers and five S.79 bombers, all from 34° *Gruppo*, attacked Convoy ASF 21 at dusk near Kupho Island. The Italians, being fired upon by the anti-aircraft cruisers HMS *Coventry* and HMS *Carlisle*, scored no hits.

281ª *Squadriglia* finally went into action on 23 and 24 March when Capitano Buscaglia and Tenente Giorgio Sacchetti unsuccessfully targeted British shipping south of Crete. Four days later (28 March), both 34° *Gruppo* and 281ª *Squadriglia* supported the Italian fleet while it was engaged in the Gavdos naval battle. That day, between 0710 hrs and 0815 hrs, two 68ª *Squadriglia* S.79s flown by Maggiore Cannaviello and Capitano Grossi intercepted Swordfish '5F' from HMS *Formidable* while it was on a reconnaissance flight. The S.79s, which were providing air cover for the Italian warships, forced the crew of the biplane to abandon their mission.

At 1255 hrs Capitano Buscaglia's S.79, leading those of Tenenti Pietro Greco and Cimicchi, attacked Mediterranean Fleet units. A mechanical problem forced Cimicchi to turn back, but Buscaglia and Greco (the latter's S.79 being damaged by ack-ack shrapnel) launched their torpedoes at HMS *Formidable*, but the carrier successfully avoided them. That same afternoon Maggiore Cannaviello's S.79 returned to attack the Royal Navy warships, claiming a torpedo hit on a cruiser at 1733 hrs – no hit was in fact scored. The British reported that three Fulmars from *Formidable* briefly attacked Cannaviello's torpedo-bomber before it disengaged, but there is no reference to this interception in the 34° *Gruppo* war diary.

At 1345 hrs on 29 March, during the aftermath of the dramatic Battle of Cape Matapan, two 279ª *Squadriglia* S.79s flown by Capitano Orazio Bernardini and Tenente Rodolfo Guza launched their torpedoes at two British destroyers. One missed, but the other reportedly struck home. The two *Sparvieri* did not escape unscathed, however, with both aircraft being hit by defensive fire from the naval vessels.

On 2 April, at 1245 hrs, four S.79 torpedo-bombers, – two each from 281ª *Squadriglia* (flown by Tenenti Giorgio Sacchetti and Giuseppe

Tenente di Vascello Osservatore Domenico Baffigo is seen here wearing a scarf featuring the graphic 'torpedo and skull' insignia of 279ª *Squadriglia*. This valiant naval officer usually flew as observer in Capitano Bernardini's crew. Later in the war Baffigo was promoted to capitano di corvetta and given command of the *Regia Marina* cruiser *Giulio Germanico* whilst it was still under construction in Castellammare di Stabia, near Naples. Baffigo was killed by German troops on 11 September 1943 during post-armistice combat, his vessel also being scuttled by the enemy. Baffigo was posthumously awarded a *Medaglia d'Oro al Valor Militare* following his death in combat (*Italian Navy*)

281ª *Squadriglia* crews pose for the camera at Gadurra airfield in 1941. Among the pilots standing in the back row are Tenente Carlo Faggioni (extreme left), Capitano Carlo Emanuele Buscaglia (middle) and Tenente Giuseppe Cimicchi (extreme right). All were prominent *Aerosiluranti* aces. The *squadriglia* mascot in the front row was called 'Spoletta' ('detonation fuse') (*Aeronautica Militare*)

Cimicchi) and 34° *Gruppo* (flown by Maggiore Vittorio Cannaviello and Tenente Umberto Barbani), along with three S.79 bombers of 34° *Gruppo*, attacked Convoy ANF 24 south of Crete without effect. A few hours later, at dusk, Capitano Buscaglia single-handedly attacked the same convoy south of Crete, missing a 15,000-ton vessel due to poor visibility.

Three days later a new and talented pilot joined 281ª *Squadriglia* at Gadurra, although an early incident almost cost him his place in the unit. Upon returning from one of his first sorties, 26-year-old Tenente Carlo Faggioni landed side-by-side at Gadurra with Tenente Spezzaferri. Capitano Buscaglia had previously banned such landings because of the narrowness of the runway. Faggioni's bomber hit two 163ª *Squadriglia* Fiat CR.42 biplane fighters that were parked alongside the runway, damaging both of them and the S.79. This accident enraged Buscaglia, and Faggioni's S.79 career appeared to be over before it had started. However, Tenente Cimicchi, who appreciated Faggioni's skills, intervened in his favour and the young officer was given a second chance. Within several weeks Faggioni had shown his worth in combat, and he eventually became one of the most popular, and effective, officers in the unit.

On 6 April 279ª *Squadriglia* left Sicily, moving first to Grottaglie airport in Apulia and then to Gadurra on the 14th.

281ª *SQUADRIGLIA'S* FIRST SUCCESS

On 18 April 281ª *Squadriglia* scored its first confirmed success when the 7138-ton tanker *British Science,* part of Convoy AN 27, was attacked. The vessel was initially targeted at 1230 hrs by two S.79 torpedo-bombers from 279ª *Squadriglia*, the aircraft being flown by Tenenti Umberto Barbani and Angelo Caponetti, along with three S.79 bombers of 68ª *Squadriglia* (34° *Gruppo*). One torpedo struck and damaged the tanker, reducing its speed to six knots, and it headed, isolated and laboriously, for Souda Bay. At 1428 hrs, while the crippled oiler was navigating in Kasos Strait, two S.79s flown by Tenenti Cimicchi (281ª *Squadriglia*) and Orfeo Fiumani (279ª *Squadriglia*) appeared, and the former attacked. Cimicchi's torpedo hit the ship, which sank.

But the Italians paid for this success, for during the first attack Flg Off Andy Smith, flying a Blenheim IF fighter of No 30 Sqn, intercepted Barbani's aircraft and shot it down. The doomed S.79 ditched near Camilloni Island, and all of Barbani's crew, being slightly wounded, took to their dinghy. They were later picked up by an Italian rescue floatplane. Smith then attacked Caponetti's S.79 and claimed it as damaged, but return fire hit the Blenheim IF, forcing Smith to break off. The crippled British fighter forced-landed on Crete's Maleme airfield, observer Plt Off J H Strong having to extinguish an engine fire en route.

Left: Capitano Buscaglia and his crew stand in front of their S.79 281-5 on Gadurra airfield in the spring of 1941. Roughly painted fuselage numbers indicate that this trimotor was one of the original five *Sparvieri* formerly in service with 34° *Gruppo* (*Aeronautica Militare*)

The trio of S.79 bombers from 34° *Gruppo* was also intercepted by British fighters after claiming a hit on a cruiser, two 805 NAS Fulmars (one of which was flown by Sub Lt Royston Griffin) inflicting damage on all three machines.

That same afternoon, at 1820 hrs (British time), it was 279ª *Squadriglia's* turn to be engaged in combat. Two S.79s flown by Capitano Orazio Bernardini and Tenente Rodolfo Guza sighted warships of the Mediterranean Fleet, but as they were running in to attack them they were intercepted by an 803 NAS Fulmar patrol from *Formidable*. The Fulmars chased the S.79s for 20 minutes, and bursts fired by ace Sub Lt Alfred William Theobald struck Tenente Guza's aircraft, wounding the pilot and two airmen. Return fire from the trimotors was effective, however, hitting Fulmar '6J' and wounding its pilot, Lt Donald Gibson, in the arm. His crippled fighter crashed on *Formidable's* flightdeck when he attempted to land, sending it plunging into the sea. Gibson was quickly picked up by the destroyer HMS *Hereward*, but his observer, Sub Lt Peter Ashbrooke, lost his life.

On 20 April S.79 MM23876 of 281ª *Squadriglia*, flown by Tenente Carlo Faggioni, attacked Convoy AS 26 southeast of Gavdos Island. Amidst fierce ack-ack the Italian crew claimed to have torpedoed a tanker (not confirmed by the British), but the S.79 was then intercepted by a No 30 Sqn Blenheim IF flown, again, by Flg Off Smith. He fired one burst and then his guns jammed, forcing him to break off. Faggioni also disengaged, his S.79 having been hit twice by shrapnel.

The next day 34° *Gruppo Autonomo* was officially denominated *Aerosilurante*, its 67ª and 68ª *Squadriglie* being deactivated and replaced by 279ª and 281ª *Squadriglie*. 21 April also saw perhaps the most dramatic fate ever to befall an S.79. Late in the afternoon two 278ª *Squadriglia* aircraft, flown by Tenente Robone and Capitano Oscar Cimolini, took off from Berka, in Cyrenaica, at 1650 hrs and 1725 hrs, respectively, to attack Convoy AS 26 in the eastern Mediterranean. Robone claimed one hit on a 6000-ton ship, which has been identified as the 6098-ton *British Lord*, but British sources state that it was actually disabled by a bomb dropped by Ju 88s of II./LG 1. After Cimolini dropped his torpedo his S.79 failed to return, and its fate remained a mystery for 19 years.

Between 21 July and 5 October 1960, a team from an Italian petroleum company discovered both the wreck of the S.79 and the remains of its crew in the desert some 400 km (250 miles) south of Benghazi. After investigation it was ascertained that the crew of S.79 MM23881 had lost their way in the darkness due to a malfunctioning compass and radio, and had forced-landed in the desert. In the crash some crewmen sustained fractures and

Armourers of 281ª *Squadriglia* attach a torpedo to a *Sparviero* at Gadurra during the summer of 1941 (*Aeronautica Militare*)

An in-flight study of a 278ª *Squadriglia* S.79 (note the unit badge mid-fuselage) that some researchers have identified from photographic evidence as MM23881 278-3. This aircraft, flown by Capitano Cimolini, failed to return from a mission on 21 April 1941 after the crew lost its way. Cimolini eventually forced-landed in the Libyan desert 400 km (250 miles) south of Benghazi, the aircraft's wreck and the crew's bodies being discovered there 19 years later (*Bundesarchiv*)

Tenente Franco Cappa of 280ᵃ *Squadriglia* was shot down by naval anti-aircraft fire while attacking Convoy *Tiger* on 8 May 1941. Despite his aircraft having a broken wing, he managed to drop his torpedo before S.79 MM23872 280-5 crashed, killing all on board. Cappa's determination earned him a posthumous *Medaglia d'Oro al Valor Militare (Aeronautica Militare)*

A remarkable shot taken from an S.79 during the attack on Convoy *Tiger* by 280ᵃ *Squadriglia* on 8 May 1941, the unit being led on this occasion by Capitano Amedeo Mojoli (*via author*)

were unable to move. In a desperate attempt to seek assistance, gunner 1° Aviere Gianni Romanini (probably along with a comrade, whose body was never found) started a northbound march. However, the trek came to a dramatic end when, after some days marching, Romanini fell exhausted short of the Jalo–Giarabub track – his skeletal remains were discovered 19 years later.

ATTACKING THE *TIGER* CONVOY

On 8 May at 1245 hrs (Italian time) five 280ᵃ *Squadriglia* S.79s, escorted by 15 CR.42s of 3° *Gruppo Caccia*, went after Alexandria-bound convoy WS 8 (codenamed Operation *Tiger*). The convoy's freighters were carrying 295 tanks and 53 crated Hurricane fighters. Force 'H' commander Adm James Somerville later described the attackers as 'wicked looking brutes just skimming over the sea'. The *Sparvieri*, led by Capitano Mojoli, encountered fierce defence both by carrier-borne Fulmars from HMS *Ark Royal* (four each from 807 and 808 NASs) and anti-aircraft fire.

Tenente Cappa closed in on his target, looking for a certain 'kill', but a cannon shell broke a wing of his trimotor (MM23872/280-5) and sent it crashing into the sea just as it released its torpedo. All aboard were killed, but their determination earned Cappa and his crew, respectively, posthumous Gold and Silver Medals for Military Valour. During the attack *Ark Royal* managed to comb the track of the torpedoes, avoiding at least four of them. Meanwhile, the horrified Adm Somerville saw one torpedo heading straight for his flagship, HMS *Renown*. He later recalled, '"Now we're for it", I thought, but would you believe it, the damn thing finished its run and I watched it sink about ten yards from the ship'. Thus *Renown* had escaped by a whisker.

Sottotenente Marino Marini's aircraft (MM23946/280-4) was brought down by Fulmars and ditched at 1300 hrs near Galite Island. Its unharmed crew, which took to their raft and reached land, were later picked up by a Vichy French seaplane and transported to Tunis. Fulmars also repeatedly hit Capitano Mojoli's S.79 (280-2), whose gunners claimed one 'Hurricane' probably shot down. The FAA fighters in turn scored several hits on Tenente Ugo Rivoli's 280-1.

Fulmars of 808 NAS also clashed with 3° *Gruppo* CR.42s, which shot down the unit's CO, Lt R C Tillard – he was killed along with his observer, Sub Lt Mark Somerville (Adm Somerville's nephew) – and badly damaged three other fighters. Lt Giles Guthrie, flying one of the latter machines, recovered from a steep spin at low altitude and then attacked an S.79 twice before his guns failed. Two 153ᵃ *Squadriglia* CR.42s (flown by Tenenti Mancini and Mattei) were damaged. All of the shot-up Fulmars had managed to land back on *Ark Royal* by 1437 hrs (British time).

Convoy WS 8 was targeted again at 1910 hrs (Italian time) by three 278ᵃ *Squadriglia* S.79s flown by Tenenti Spezzaferri, La Guercia and Copello, whose torpedoes missed *Renown* and *Ark Royal*. Two 808

An S.79 from 281ª *Squadriglia* is taxied out at the start of a mission from Gadurra during mid 1941 (*Aeronautica Militare*)

NAS Fulmars had scrambled to intercept the S.79s at 2015 hrs (British time), but aces Lts Giles Guthrie and Ronnie Hay failed to prevent the attack. Despite the S.79s being damaged by anti-aircraft shell splinters, none were lost – two landed at Pantelleria while Copello flew to Sciacca. Tenente Guido Robone's S.79, which was the fourth aircraft assigned to this mission, was forced to abort the initial attack when it suffered engine trouble. Robone and his crew boldly took off again at 2245 hrs and pressed home their attack at around midnight. Amidst anti-aircraft crossfire Robone launched his torpedo at the battleship HMS *Queen Elizabeth*, which narrowly evaded it, then returned to base.

In the Aegean at 1825 hrs that same day three 281ª *Squadriglia* (34° *Gruppo*) S.79s piloted by Capitano Buscaglia and Tenenti Pietro Greco and Carlo Faggioni, successfully attacked Convoy AN 30, although they were all damaged by anti-aircraft fire. The British 4998-ton motor vessel *Rawnsley*, hit by one torpedo, was taken in tow by the Royal Australian Navy destroyer HMAS *Waterhen* and later stranded in Hierapetra Bay, off southern Crete, where, on the night of 12 May, it was sunk by German bombers.

Also on 8 May 279ª *Squadriglia* left 34° *Gruppo* and became autonomous again, returning to Benghazi K2 airfield. Here, it transferred some of its personnel to 281ª *Squadriglia* including pilots Tenenti Barbani and Massera and observer Tenente di Vascello Riva. On 27 May 279ª *Squadriglia* moved to El Fteiah airfield, near Derna.

The CO of 34° *Gruppo* at this time was Maggiore Vittorio Cannaviello, who was also a torpedo-bomber enthusiast. He studied the best use of aerial torpedoes, testing them and taking care of his crews' training. During the evening of 20 May two *Sparvieri* torpedo-bombers of 281ª *Squadriglia*, flown by Cannaviello and Capitano Guglielmo Di Luise, attacked the British Force 'C' (comprising the cruisers HMS *Naiad* and HMAS *Perth* and four destroyers) southwest of Crete. The Italians claimed that both of their torpedoes had struck a 10,000-ton cruiser, but this was not confirmed by the British. The furious anti-aircraft defence damaged Di Luise's aircraft.

Altogether, from 10 January to 22 May 1941, Italian torpedo-bombers had launched 46 torpedoes against ships in open sea, losing seven aircraft in the process.

A military awards ceremony at Rhodes in 1941. Seated is flight engineer Sergente Maggiore Nicola Gaeta, who was part of Tenente Faggioni's crew during the action over Cyprus on 4 July 1941. He remained firmly at his post despite being wounded, Gaeta's left leg subsequently having to be amputated. Decorated with the Silver Medal for Military Valour for his bravery, Gaeta resumed flying with AR's *Gruppo* 'Buscaglia'. Sadly, he was killed in combat with 57th FG Thunderbolts on 6 April 1944. Standing behind Gaeta, from left to right, are pilots Capitano Buscaglia, Tenente Faggioni and Sergente Maggiore Ugo Scardapane (*Aeronautica Militare*)

ATTACKING CYPRUS AND TOBRUK SUPPLY ROUTES

On 24 June 1941 Italian reconnaissance aircraft spotted a small Tobruk-bound convoy that had sailed from Alexandria – it comprised the tanker *Pass of Balmaha* along with the sloops HMS *Auckland* and HMAS *Parramatta*. At 1045 hrs these ships were attacked, to no avail, by two 279ª *Squadriglia* S.79 torpedo-bombers piloted by Capitano Orazio Bernardini and Tenente Mario Frongia. The Italian aircraft were intercepted by Hurricane Is of No 274 Sqn, one of which, flown by Flg Off Joe Hobbs, shot down *Sparviero* MM23860 of Capitano Bernardini, wounding all the crew apart from co-pilot Sergente Maggiore Urbano Gentilini, who sustained only light splinter grazes.

Aboard the downed S.79, the bursts of fire from the Hurricane had badly wounded Maresciallo Armiere Vito Sinisi and Sergente Maggiore Marconista Riccardo Balagna. Both airmen succumbed to their wounds prior to the downed aircrew being picked up by a Cant Z.506 rescue floatplane hours later. Sinisi and Balagna were posthumously awarded the Gold Medal for Military Valour for their bravery.

Throughout July 1941 281ª *Squadriglia* continuously flew missions and patrols against enemy ships sailing between Cyprus and the Egyptian coast. On the 1st the unit regained its autonomous status, thus leaving 34° *Gruppo* to officially deactivate between 30 June and 3 July. On 4 July Capitano Buscaglia and Tenenti Faggioni, Cimicchi and Mazzilli claimed two torpedo hits on a 7000-ton auxiliary cruiser off Famagusta, Cyprus. In this action flight engineer Sergente Maggiore Nicola Gaeta aboard Faggioni's S.79 (MM23876) remained in his position despite suffering grave wounds to his left leg. The limb was subsequently amputated, and Gaeta was awarded the Silver Medal for Military Valour.

Buscaglia and Faggioni returned to Famagusta Bay on 7 and 9 July, but failed to hit any of the vessels they attacked. Following the second of these missions both aircraft (Buscaglia's MM23838 and Faggioni's MM23960) returned to base badly battle-damaged. On 19 July Buscaglia (in the repaired MM23838) and Faggioni (in MM23876) reported hitting a 10,000-ton cruiser off Mersa Matruh. Again, both *Sparvieri* were damaged by anti-aircraft fire.

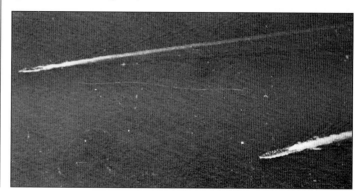

Two British warships are seen at full speed whilst under attack by 281ª *Squadriglia Sparvieri* off Mersa Matruh on 19 July 1941. In this action Capitano Buscaglia's S.79 MM23838 and Tenente Faggioni's MM23876 were damaged by shrapnel from naval fire (*Aeronautica Militare*)

From 22 to 24 July the S.79s of 280ª and 283ª *Squadriglie*, based at Elmas, in Sardinia, along with 278ª *Squadriglia* from Sicily, made a series of attacks on Malta-bound Convoy GM 1 (Operation *Substance*), scoring three torpedo hits for three S.79s lost. On the morning of 23 July at 0910 hrs six S.79s of 283ª *Squadriglia*, led by Capitano Giorgio Grossi, with observer Tenente di Vascello Antonio Forni aboard, and two from 280ª *Squadriglia* (Capitano Mojoli's 280-4 and Tenente Mario

S.79 '5' is made ready for action at Gadurra during the summer of 1941. According to some sources, this aircraft was one of the five *Sparvieri* that formerly served with 34° *Gruppo* from November 1940. If this is indeed the case, the aircraft subsequently saw combat with 68ª *Squadriglia* and 281ª *Squadriglia* (*Aeronautica Militare*)

Anselmi's 280-5) attacked the convoy. The defending Fulmars from *Ark Royal's* 807 and 808 NASs were distracted by 15 high-level bombers (ten S.79s of 32° *Stormo* and five Cant Z.1007bis of 51° *Gruppo*) and by the two 280ª *Squadriglia* S.79s. This allowed six 283ª *Squadriglia Sparvieri* to attack at low level.

Although three of the six attackers were repelled by the Fulmars, the remaining torpedo-bombers closed on the ships. The S.79 piloted by Tenente Roberto Cipriani dropped a torpedo, which missed. Then the *Sparviero* of Tenente Bruno Pandolfi released its weapon, which struck the destroyer HMS *Fearless*. Badly damaged by the resulting explosion, the vessel had 25 members of its crew killed. Pandolfi's S.79 was shot down by anti-aircraft fire from the stricken destroyer moments after it had released its torpedo, the downed crew being captured by the destroyer HMS *Avon Vale*. *Fearless* was later scuttled by a torpedo fired at 1055 hrs by the destroyer HMS *Forester*.

The third, and last, S.79, flown by Tenente Francesco 'Ciccio' Di Bella, launched a torpedo that badly damaged the cruiser HMS *Manchester* (35 crewmen were killed and 39 wounded)', and the vessel was out of service for nine months. For this action Di Bella was decorated with his second Silver Medal for Military Valour in the field.

Ark Royal's Fulmars claimed two S.79 bombers downed and two damaged (32° *Stormo's* two *Gruppi* reported one lost and six damaged) during this engagement, although effective defensive fire from *Sparvieri* gunners saw them shoot down three FAA fighters. 283ª *Squadriglia* crews

This in-flight photograph of S.79 '5' was taken on 23 July 1941. That day, during Operation *Substance*, Tenente Bruno Pandolfi of 283ª *Squadriglia* sank the destroyer HMS *Fearless* while Tenente Francesco Di Bella of the same unit seriously damaged the cruiser HMS *Manchester* (*Aeronautica Militare*)

claimed a Fulmar destroyed and a second example as a probable.

After takeoff at 1620 hrs three 280ª *Squadriglia Sparvieri* flown by Capitano Mojoli (280-5) and Tenenti Ugo Rivoli (280-1) and Alessandro Setti (280-6) attacked, but missed, HMS *Manchester* and HMS *Avon Vale*. Then, at 1645 hrs, four 283ª *Squadriglia* S.79s, led by Capitano Grossi, again with Tenente di Vascello Forni as observer, were

On 30 July 1941 the Aegean Islands Governor, *Ammiraglio di Squadra* Campioni, along with *Generale di Brigata Aerea* Ulisse Longo, AOC *Aeronautica Egeo*, visited 281ª *Squadriglia* at Gadurra airfield. Here, Capitano Buscaglia leads the two high-ranking officers reviewing the unit's aircraft (*Aeronautica Militare*)

The Norwegian tanker *Hoegh Hood* takes a torpedo hit on 24 July 1941. This ship was attacked at around 1730 hrs that afternoon by two 280ª *Squadriglia Sparvieri* flown by Capitano Amedeo Mojoli and Tenente Ugo Rivoli (*Aeronautica Militare*)

intercepted by three 808 NAS Fulmars flown by Lt Ronnie Hay, Sub Lt Alan Goodfellow and PO Dennis Taylor. The British trio shot down the S.79 of Tenente Dolfus, whose crew was later captured by the destroyer HMS *Foresight*. Two other S.79s were also damaged and five airmen wounded by the Fulmars. One of the damaged *Sparvieri* was Capitano Grossi's aircraft, which was attacked by all three British pilots – Grossi himself was wounded.

Tenente Cipriani's trimotor was also badly hit, and the crew ditched near Cape Carbonara. They were picked up by a Savoia-Marchetti S.66 rescue flying boat from 613ª *Squadriglia*. Lts Edgar Lewin and Giles Guthrie of 808 NAS also claimed S.79 victories near Sardinia.

At 1900 hrs four *Sparvieri* of 278ª *Squadriglia* (led by Capitano Magagnoli), after missing the cruisers HMS *Edinburgh* and HMS *Hermione*, were bounced by Beaufighters of No 272 Sqn, one of which, T3304 flown by Sgts W M Deakin and C F Jenkins, was shot down by the escorting CR.42 fighters of 23° *Gruppo*.

The next day (24 July) *Sparvieri* continued to harass the convoy. The first was a lone S.79 of 278ª *Squadriglia*, flown by Capitano Mario Spezzaferri, whose torpedo missed the steamer *Sydney Star* at 0937 hrs – the ship had already been damaged by MAS (*Motoscafo armato silurante* – torpedo-armed motorboats) boats the previous night. After the attack Spezzaferri's S.79 was chased, to no avail, by a No 272 Sqn Beaufighter. In the late morning three 280ª *Squadriglia* S.79s flown by Tenenti Anselmi (280-5), Rivoli (280-1) and Setti (280-4) targeted the merchantmen *Amerika* and *Thermopylae* from the Gibraltar-bound convoy MG 1, but to no avail. Finally, at around 1730 hrs, a torpedo dropped by one of two 280ª *Squadriglia* S.79s flown by Capitano Mojoli (280-6) and Tenente Rivoli (280-1) damaged the 9351-ton Norwegian tanker *Hoegh Hood*, although the vessel still made it to Gibraltar. Tenente Setti's 280-4 missed the steamer *Settler* at around this time too.

Although the Italians had successfully challenged the *Substance* convoy, inflicting losses, the British managed to get precious supplies through to Malta via other convoys.

And S.79 crews had no rest even when on the ground, as Malta-based Beaufighters started to harass them in their 'nests'. On 30 July six No 272 Sqn aircraft strafed Elmas airfield at 1220 hrs, Sqn Ldr Andrew Fletcher and Flt Lt Campbell badly damaging 283ª *Squadriglia* S.79 MM23948 and wounding nine groundcrew from other units.

On 1 August two new pilots, Tenente Giulio Cesare Graziani and Sottotenente Aldo Forzinetti, were posted to 281ᵃ *Squadriglia*. Both men would soon be in the vanguard of the action in what proved to be an intense month for the *Aerosiluranti*. On the 6th Capitano Buscaglia, Tenente Graziani and Sottotenente Forzinetti attacked two destroyers off Mersa Matruh, claiming hits on both. Five days later the same trio of pilots were again at work, with Buscaglia torpedoing the 2900-ton netlayer HMS *Protector* off Port Said. Two crewmen were killed and three wounded aboard the British ship, which was put out of service for the rest of the war.

The British netlayer HMS *Protector* on 11 August 1941, photographed from one of the 281ᵃ *Squadriglia* S.79s that attacked it. A torpedo dropped by Capitano Buscaglia's MM23877 hit the vessel, causing such damage that the ship was out of commission for 48 months (*Aeronautica Militare*)

There were other changes among 281ᵃ *Squadriglia* personnel during the course of the month. On the 18th Tenente Luigi Rovelli was posted in, while Tenenti Greco and Mazzilli were transferred to other units.

On 20 August, 81 miles north of Port Said, Tenente Graziani and Sottotenente Forzinetti attacked the 4782-ton tanker *Turbo* which, badly crippled by a torpedo, was towed to Port Said and eventually sank on 5 April 1942. The graphic report on this action in the 281ᵃ *Squadriglia* war diary seemingly credits the *Turbo*'s torpedoing to Forzinetti.

Twenty-four hours prior to this action Capitano Amedeo Mojoli (posted to 30° *Stormo*) handed over command of 280ᵃ *Squadriglia* to Capitano Franco Melley.

Between 19 and 29 August *Regia Aeronautica* and Luftwaffe units harassed British warships engaged in Operation *Treacle* – the replacement of the Tobruk garrison's 9th Australian Division units with Polish Carpathian Brigade and British 70th Division troops.

At 1845 hrs on the 19th a single 279ᵃ *Squadriglia* S.79, flown by Capitano Giulio Marini, attacked three destroyers, unsuccessfully launching a torpedo at one of them that the crew had identified as a 1690-ton *Jervis* class vessel. Naval anti-aircraft fire slightly damaged the starboard engine of Marini's aircraft.

Buscaglia, Graziani and Forzinetti took off at 1030 hrs on 21 August, and at 1225 hrs they sighted three destroyers west of Alexandria, attacking them between 1227-1228 hrs. British reports record that the destroyers HMS *Kandahar*, HMS *Griffin* and HMS *Jackal* were engaged that day. The destroyers, which put up a fierce, though delayed, barrage, were not hit, and returned to Alexandria the next day. On their return trip at 1310 hrs, the S.79s were attacked by two Blenheim fighters, which were repelled by the *Sparvieris'* defensive fire. The three S.79s landed safely back at Gadurra at 1435 hrs.

The British tanker *Turbo* was set ablaze by a single torpedo during an attack by Tenente Graziani and Sottotenente Forzinetti of 281ᵃ *Squadriglia* on 20 August 1941 (*Aeronautica Militare*)

One of the three destroyers attacked by 281ª *Squadriglia* on 21 August 1941 is seen from the dorsal position of an S.79 during the aircraft's escape manoeuvre. Note the arrowhead-shaped device fitted at left to prevent the *Sparviero's* tail from being damaged by rounds fired from the aircraft's own dorsal gun (*Aeronautica Militare*)

Tenente Pietro Donà delle Rose, the young Venetian nobleman pilot of 283ª *Squadriglia*, was killed on 27 August 1941 whilst trying to draw fire from the gunners aboard the steamer *Deucalion*. This daring act earned him the posthumous award of the *Medaglia d'Oro al Valor Militare* (*Aeronautica Militare*)

On 27 August at 2014 hrs (Italian time), an S.79 of 279ª *Squadriglia*, flown by Capitano Giulio Marini, targeted the 5450-ton cruiser HMS *Phoebe* 27 miles north of Bardia. The Royal Navy reported that the ship was hit at 2120 hrs (British time, another source stating 2145 hrs) by one torpedo on the starboard side under 'Q' gun deck, killing eight ratings and putting the ship out of commission for eight months. In October 1941 the cruiser left the Mediterranean for Brooklyn Navy Yard, New York, where from November 1941 it underwent lengthy repairs, before returning to England in May 1942.

27 August had also seen the British 7516-ton steamship *Deucalion* attacked as it tried to reach Gibraltar, having sailed from Malta the previous day. On the morning of the 27th the Italians sighted the vessel off the Algerian coast, and at 1315 hrs two 280ª *Squadriglia* S.79s flown by Capitano Franco Melley (280-2) and Tenente Mario Giacopinelli (280-3) took off from Sardinia to attack it. The ship was spotted westbound near Galite Island and attacked, whereupon it zigzagged swiftly to evade the torpedoes dropped by the S.79s. Unfortunately for the Italians Melley's torpedo passed under the ship's hull, while Giacopinelli's struck the target but failed to explode.

Not only had the British steamer had a lucky escape, both aircraft had been repeatedly hit by the fierce anti-aircraft fire. The two S.79s returned to base, from where, at 1625 hrs, two more torpedo-bombers, flown by Tenente Pietro Donà delle Rose of 283ª *Squadriglia* and Tenente Alessandro Setti of 280ª *Squadriglia*, got airborne. Before takeoff the Italian aircrews had planned a means of achieving success. Donà delle Rose would distract *Deucalion*'s ack-ack by attacking the ship head-on and forcing it to slow down, while Setti (in 280-8) would attack the steamer from the side. Donà, a descendant of an ancient and wealthy Venetian family who had given at least three *Dogi* (Dukes) to the Republic of Venice, was determined to achieve victory at any price.

The two S.79s spotted the British vessel about 40 miles north of Cape Bougaroun, in eastern Algeria, and split up to carry out their attack. Donà delle Rose made his head-on attack, forcing the *Deucalion* to reduce speed. Meanwhile, as Setti was positioning for his attack, the ship's captain displayed some uncertainty about how to evade, thus presenting an ideal target. Donà's aircraft was straddled by the violent anti-aircraft fire, being hit fatally just a few hundred metres from the ship just as Setti dropped his torpedo at close range. The weapon struck but did not explode, scraping along the ship's hull. This was both an heroic and sad conclusion to a well-synchronised action. Donà's aircraft crashed in the sea short of *Deucalion*, killing all of its crew. The British reported that one of the torpedoes (probably that dropped by Donà) had missed the ship by 100 m (100 yds). Although Setti's *Sparviero* was damaged by anti-aircraft fire it made it back to base at 1950 hrs.

The next day *Sparvieri* from both *squadriglie* searched for the downed aircraft but only saw a body kept afloat by a lifejacket. There were no signs of survivors. An Italian submarine picked up the body, identified as that of observer Tenente di Vascello Antonio Forni, who was uninjured but had died of exposure.

Apart from bad luck, this action underlined yet again the gallantry and determination displayed by Italian torpedo airmen. Both Tenente Pietro Donà delle Rose and Tenente di Vascello Antonio Forni were posthumously decorated with the Gold Medal for Military Valour.

Deucalion reached Gibraltar two days later, on the 29th, but its appointment with destiny had only been delayed. The ship's luck ran out on 12 August 1942 when it was sunk north of Bizerte by He 111 torpedo-bombers of *Staffel* 6./KG 26 during the bloody Operation *Pedestal*.

HALBERD CONVOY

1 September 1941 was significant for the *Aerosiluranti*, as it was the date on which the first torpedo-bomber group was formed. The new large unit (based at Elmas, in Sardinia), designated 130° *Gruppo Autonomo AS*, comprised the already autonomous 280ª and 283ª *Squadriglie*.

On 27 September nine *Sparvieri* of 130° *Gruppo*, reinforced by two others from 278ª *Squadriglia* (flown by Tenenti Venturini and Bucceri) that had reached Elmas from Sicily on the 26th, left the airfield at 1150 hrs to attack the large Malta-bound Convoy GM 2 (Operation *Halberd*). Three 280ª *Squadriglia* S.79s (Capitano Melley in 280-6 and Tenenti Setti and Giacopinelli in 280-1 and 280-8, respectively) attacked the escort screen on the convoy's port flank at around 1345 hrs, narrowly missing the destroyer HMS *Lightning*. Anti-aircraft fire from *Ark Royal* and the battleship HMS *Nelson* shot down 280ª *Squadriglia* S.79 MM24077 280-7 of Tenente Carlo Deslex, killing all onboard. While making their escape at 1358 hrs, the two 278ª *Squadriglia* S.79s, which had attacked along with Deslex, were chased and damaged by *Ark Royal's* Fulmars.

Naval fire forced the five 283ª *Squadriglia* S.79s, led by Capitano Grossi and including Tenente 'Ciccio' Di Bella's aircraft, back to base at 1530 hrs. Two Blenheims that were busy strafing Elmas when the S.79s returned also attacked Tenente Barioglio's aircraft as it was landing, but the pilot disengaged and reached Decimomannu at 1610 hrs. Capitano Grossi's five-strong patrol took off again at 1810 hrs and tried another attack on the convoy when it was ten miles north of Zembra at around 2000 hrs. Amidst accurate naval fire, Grossi and Tenenti Cipriani and Barioglio launched torpedoes at some cruisers, but to no avail. All three aircraft

Tenente di Vascello Antonio Forni took part as an observer in the battle over the *Substance* convoy, and subsequently lost his life aboard Tenente Donà delle Rose's S.79 while attacking the *Deucalion*. He too was posthumously awarded the *Medaglia d'Oro al Valor Militare* (*Aeronautica Militare*)

This dramatic photograph, taken during one of several Malta-bound convoys that was targeted by the *Sparvieri* in the summer of 1941, shows an S.79 flying low between a British battleship and a carrier spearheading the convoy (*Aeronautica Militare*)

During the *Halberd* battle Capitano Dante Magagnoli, CO of 278ª *Squadriglia*, fatally torpedoed the large British transport *Imperial Star*, which had to be scuttled shortly thereafter (*via author*)

Capitano Buscaglia (left) chats with two other prominent pilots from 281ª *Squadriglia*, Tenenti Giuseppe Cipelletti (centre, with the unit from 27 October 1941) and Giuseppe Cimicchi (right) (*SME*)

returned to Decimomannu at 2150 hrs, Barioglio's S.79 having been slightly damaged by shrapnel.

A short while later Tenente Francesco Di Bella twice failed to launch his torpedo owing to a faulty release mechanism, returning to base at 2250 hrs. Tenente Guido Focacci, meanwhile, lost sight of the convoy and made it back to 'Decimo' at 2325 hrs with his torpedo still attached.

Three hours earlier, at 2030 hrs, two S.79s from 278ª *Squadriglia* flown by Capitano Dante Magagnoli and Tenente Lelio Silva, had taken off from Elmas and made a surprise attack on the convoy. Magagnoli torpedoed the 12,427-ton merchant ship *Imperial Star*, which had to be scuttled by the destroyer HMS *Oribi*. While trying to avoid the torpedoes the *City of Calcutta* and *Rowallan Castle* collided, sustaining serious damage, but both were able to continue.

Tenenti Di Bella, Focacci and Francesco Belloni of 283ª *Squadriglia* went after the convoy once again the following day. At 1830 hrs, near Galite Island, they attacked the empty steamers *City of Pretoria* and *Port Chalmers*, but the ship avoided all torpedoes. Despite his persistent bad luck, Di Bella was subsequently awarded his third Silver Medal for Military Valour for his work from September to December 1941.

The *Sparvieri* on their Sardinian bases were always being harassed by the Beaufighters of No 272 Sqn, and on 28 September Sqn Ldr Andrew Fletcher and Flg Off Norman Lee claimed, respectively, two and one S.79s probably shot down near Cagliari airfield. The next day No 272 Sqn's Beaufighters were again in action, strafing Elmas. Fletcher claimed three S.79s destroyed on the ground, but the Italians recorded only one machine slightly damaged. The British reported this action as taking place on the 30th.

On 13 October, 20 miles northwest of Alexandria, Tenenti Giulio Cesare Graziani and Carlo Faggioni boldly attacked the battleships *Queen Elizabeth* and HMS *Barham*. Their compatriot, Tenente Giuseppe Cimicchi, targeted a cruiser. Although all their torpedoes missed, Graziani audaciously flew over *Barham* at low level, and his S.79's starboard wing was damaged by the battleship's gunfire. Graziani managed to return to Rhodes in his crippled aircraft following a flight of more 300 miles – a feat that earned him official praise from the highest military authorities. He later recalled the episode as follows;

'I passed low over the battleship *Barham*'s turrets. I can still hear in my ears the four-barrelled guns "shelling their rosary" at my aircraft, which, incredibly, remained unscathed. When I found myself on the other side, among the cruisers' and destroyers' shell bursts, things got worse. The aircraft was shaken by the shock waves of the cannon shells exploding all around, until I felt a blow on the right wing, from which some fragments flew off.'

This action earned Graziani, Cimicchi and Faggioni the Silver

Medal for Military Valour. Later, for his daring attack (and for an action over East Africa on 16 December 1940) Graziani was awarded the Gold Medal for Military Valour. This was remarkable because it was presented to a living pilot at a time when the award was usually presented posthumously.

On 22 October four 279ª *Squadriglia* S.79s led by Capitano Orazio Bernardini left El Fteiah airfield at 1710 hrs in search of enemy ships reported north of Ras Azzaz. The vessels were not found, but Tenente Umberto Barbani's aircraft failed to return.

TORPEDOING ISOLATED FREIGHTERS

During the final months of 1941 the British adopted the stratagem of sending lone freighters disguised as neutral ships to the besieged island of Malta. Unfortunately for the Allies, the Italian response to this tactic proved to be one of the few occasions when torpedo-bomber operations were really effective. For example, on 24 October three S.79s of 130° *Gruppo* (two from 280ª *Squadriglia*, namely Capitano Melley's 280-3 and Sottotenente Caresio's 280-9, and Tenente Guido Focacci of 283ª *Squadriglia*) attacked the 5720-ton British freighter *Empire Guillemot* west of Galite Island. The ship was hit aft at 1400 hrs by a torpedo dropped by the *Sparviero* of Tenente Focacci, and it sank 30 miles off Las Rosas some 40 minutes later. Caresio did not drop his torpedo, and all three S.79s returned at 1520 hrs.

On 14 November 130° *Gruppo* struck again when Tenente Camillo Barioglio of 283ª *Squadriglia* scored another success for his unit, torpedoing and sinking the 6463-ton steamship *Empire Pelican* 25 miles east of Galite Island. After suffering further losses to S.84 torpedo-bombers and Italian minefields, the British finally ended the experiment, reverting to the safer convoy system.

Three days earlier, Capitano Ugo Rivoli had left 130° *Gruppo* for 278ª *Squadriglia*, where he replaced Capitano Dante Magagnoli as the unit's CO.

On 23 November 281ª *Squadriglia* again scored against enemy shipping. North of Mersa Matruh, Capitano Buscaglia and Tenente Rovelli attacked the 9871-ton troopship HMS *Glenroy*, which, badly damaged by a torpedo, was later run aground to avoid it sinking. The S.79s were intercepted by two FAA Martlets flown by Sub Lts Routley and Walsh, who fired on them for at least 16 minutes. Although they were damaged, both *Sparvieri* returned to Gadurra at 1830 hrs after a flight lasting more than four hours.

That same day 130° *Gruppo* began its Libyan operational tour, flying from Castel Benito and Misurata. On 28 November a fragmentation bomb destroyed S.79 283-1 at Castel Benito during a British air raid at 2100 hrs. On 19 December, near Castel Benito, Tenente Guido Focacci of 283ª *Squadriglia* escaped disaster when his S.79 belly-landed on bumpy

An impressive shot of the ill-fated battleship HMS *Barham*, taken by photographer 1° Aviere Tommaso Di Paolo from Tenente Graziani's 281ª *Squadriglia* S.79 as it boldly overflew the British warship during the action of 13 October 1941 (*Aeronautica Militare*)

Two S.79s possibly from 281ª *Squadriglia* attack a British battleship (almost certainly HMS *Barham*) in a photograph showing (according to some sources) the 281ª *Squadriglia* action of 13 October 1941 against the battleships HMS *Queen Elizabeth* and HMS *Barham*. If this astonishing action photograph is indeed genuine, the S.79 in the background (darting between the battleship and the torpedo-dropping *Sparviero* to right) was flown by Tenente Cimicchi

The British troopship HMS *Glenroy* is targeted by 281ᵃ *Squadriglia* S.79s on 23 November 1941. This snapshot was taken from the cockpit of one of the attacking *Sparvieri*. *Glenroy* was torpedoed and damaged by Capitano Buscaglia and Tenente Rovelli (*Aeronautica Militare*)

Capitano Giulio Marini's S.79 MM23964 279-1, crippled after the action of 1 December 1941 when 279ᵃ *Squadriglia Sparvieri* badly damaged the destroyer HMS *Jackal* (*Aeronautica Militare*)

ground with its torpedo still attached. The 130° *Gruppo* detachment operated in Libya until its repatriation on 28 December.

On 1 December three S.79 torpedo-bombers of 279ᵃ *Squadriglia*, led by Capitano Giulio Marini, with Sottotenenti Aligi Strani and Giuseppe Coci, attacked the destroyers HMS *Jackal*, HMS *Jervis*, HMS *Jaguar* and HMS *Kipling* north of Tobruk. At 1235 hrs the *Sparvieri* trio badly damaged the 1690-ton *Jackal* off Mersa Luch, putting it out of commission for five months. The Italians did not escape unscathed, however, as defensive fire damaged the starboard undercarriage and wing of Marini's trimotor (MM23964/279-1), which caused it to yaw on landing at 1330 hrs. Sottotenente Stroni's aircraft received one bullet strike between the central engine and the cockpit.

On 5 December the first Alexandria-bound convoy, TA 1, left Tobruk, and was separately attacked at around 2135 hrs by three S.79s (flown by Capitano Massimiliano Erasi of 284ᵃ *Squadriglia* and Tenente Guglielmo Ranieri and Sottotenente Alfredo Pulzetti of 279ᵃ *Squadriglia*). North of Mersa Luch the 3033-ton armed boarding ship *Chakdina* eluded a torpedo dropped by Capitano Erasi, but then a weapon launched by Tenente Ranieri struck home. Although *Chakdina* sank in just three minutes, two-thirds of the 300 Commonwealth troops and 100 Axis prisoners of war (mostly Italians) that went into the water were saved by the British destroyer HMS *Ferndale* and the trawler HMS *Thorgrim*. Among the survivors was German General Johann von Ravenstein.

At 0750 hrs on 10 December single S.79s from 284ᵃ *Squadriglia* (flown by Capitano Erasi) and 279ᵃ *Squadriglia* took off to attack the cruiser HMS *Naiad* and several destroyers north of Ras el Tin, the vessels having been shelling the Derna area. The ships greeted the *Sparvieri* with a violent barrage, and although Erasi claimed that he had probably hit *Naiad*, he had not done so.

The following day 281ᵃ *Squadriglia* divided its six aircraft up into two sections. Buscaglia, Faggioni and Forzinetti flew their S.79s to Libya, while Cimicchi, Rovelli and Cipelletti remained at Gadurra. Cimicchi acted as senior officer, as Graziani was on leave in Italy at the time. The Cimicchi-led section was the first to see action, attacking a naval force (comprising the cruisers *Naiad*, HMS *Euryalus* and HMS *Carlisle*, escorted by eight destroyers) led by Rear Adm Philip Vian south of Crete on 14 December. The torpedo-bombers were unable to press home their attacks, however, owing to good

weather and the fierce barrage put up by the warships. The manoeuvrability of the latter also enabled them to be positioned with their bows facing the attacking trimotors.

Three days later, at 1200 hrs, the trio of 281ᵃ *Squadriglia* machines in Cyrenaica took off to attack the fast transport *Breconshire*, escorted by a force of cruisers and destroyers, north of Benghazi. During this action the warships put up a formidable barrage, shooting down S.79 MM23960 and killing all of its crew. Pilot Sottotenente Aldo Forzinetti was posthumously awarded the Gold Medal for Military Valour. Buscaglia and Faggioni tried to avenge their fallen companion, launching their torpedoes at a cruiser, but without effect. The next day the two surviving S.79s were flown back to Rhodes.

The same naval formation unsuccessfully attacked by Buscaglia's patrol was also targeted by three 279ᵃ *Squadriglia* S.79s at 1755 hrs on 17 December. These *Sparvieri*, flown by Capitano Giulio Marini and Tenenti Mario Frongia and Guglielmo Ranieri, launched their torpedoes again apparently without success.

South of Crete on 28 December, four 281ᵃ *Squadriglia* S.79s flown by Capitano Buscaglia and Tenenti Cimicchi, Cipelletti and Rovelli attacked Convoy ME 8, comprising the four steamers *Clan Ferguson*, *Sydney Star*, *Ajax* and *City of Calcutta*, escorted by the cruisers HMS *Dido* and HMS *Ajax* and six destroyers. There were also some land-based 805 NAS Martlets providing air cover. During this action Tenente Luigi Rovelli's S.79 (MM24089) was shot down, all of the crew being killed. The cause of Rovelli's loss is uncertain. According to the Italians the aircraft was downed by naval fire, but the British credited Martlet pilot Lt Royston Griffin with its demise, although he was in turn shot down and killed by the *Sparviero*'s return fire. Whatever the case, Rovelli was awarded the third (second posthumous) Gold Medal for Military Valour earned by 281ᵃ *Squadriglia* pilots in 1941. Rovelli's fallen crewmen were posthumously awarded the Silver Medal for Military Valour. Altogether, 26 airmen of the unit had received Silver Medals for Military Valour that year.

This proved to be the last major action of the year for 281ᵃ *Squadriglia*, whose crews had sunk or disabled five ships and shot down one aircraft. During 1941 the *Aerosiluranti* had claimed nine warships and 30 freighters hit. Of the 260 S.79s to see combat, 14 had been lost and a further 46 damaged.

On 17 December 1941 Sottotenente Aldo Forzinetti of 281ᵃ *Squadriglia* was shot down and killed with his crew by anti-aircraft fire from the transport HMS *Breconshire*'s naval escorts. This valiant officer received a posthumous *Medaglia d'Oro al Valor Militare* (*Aeronautica Militare*)

281ᵃ *Squadriglia*'s Capitano Buscaglia and his crew. The latter are, from left to right, flight engineer Sergente Maggiore Dante Scaramucci, co-pilot Maresciallo Pasquale Di Gennaro, Capitano Carlo Emanuele Buscaglia, wireless operator Sergente Maggiore Luigi Venuti and gunner 1° Aviere Antonio Mataluna. Buscaglia and this crew fought in at least ten actions between 4 July and 28 December 1941 (*Aeronautica Militare*)

1942 – A YEAR OF BATTLES

At the start of 1942 281ª *Squadriglia* was officially disbanded, some of its personnel subsequently being posted to 205ª *Squadriglia* of 41° *Gruppo* – a unit recently converted to the torpedo-bomber role. The *gruppo* CO was Tenente Colonnello Ettore Muti, who was not only part of the Fascist Party hierarchy but also a highly decorated officer. At the time he was a living recipient of the *Medaglia d'Oro* and a veteran of the Abyssinian and Spanish wars. Muti was admired by all for his legendary boldness in action.

On 19 January at 0830 hrs an S.79 piloted by Tenente Carlo Faggioni attacked a small British convoy west of Alexandria to no avail. One week later five *Sparvieri* (three from 279ª *Squadriglia* and two from 284ª *Squadriglia*) attacked the steamer *Rowallan Castle* and the transport *Glengyle* without effect. The 279ª *Squadriglia* S.79s were flown by Capitano Giulio Marini and Tenenti Aligi Strani and Alfredo Pulzetti, while the 284ª *Squadriglia* pair were piloted by Tenente Balzarotti and Sottotenente Teta.

On 5 February Tenenti Graziani and Cimicchi attacked a Tobruk-bound oiler escorted by at least seven destroyers. The British defensive fire killed photographer 1° Aviere Tommaso Di Paolo and wounded three other crewmen aboard Graziani's *Sparviero*. Shocked, but unscathed, Graziani, with fragments of Di Paolo's brain splashed on his neck, made it back to Rhodes after a very difficult flight, with his torpedo still in place due to a damaged release mechanism.

Four days later two 205ª *Squadriglia* S.79s, flown by Tenente Ardito Cristiani and Sottotenente Dorando Cionni, took off at 1340 hrs and claimed two torpedo hits on a 6000-ton auxiliary cruiser near Mersa Matruh. Despite violent ack-ack both *Sparvieri* returned at 1750 hrs.

Significant results were achieved on 15 February when two 205ª *Squadriglia* S.79s (flown by Capitano Marino Marini and Sottotenente Saverio Mayer) attacked Malta Convoy MW 9 during its return to Egypt. The Italians were intercepted by Hurricanes of No 30 Sqn and Beaufighters of No 252 Sqn. Sgts

The legendary Tenente Colonnello Ettore Muti, CO of 41° *Gruppo*, is seen here at the controls of his trimotor. He had been awarded the *Medaglia d'Oro al Valor Militare* for his outstanding courage in Spain during the Civil War. Some former 281ª *Squadriglia* pilots served under him after their unit's temporary disbandment in early 1942 (*via author*)

Richard Marrack, Bate and Lawrence of No 30 Sqn claimed an S.79 destroyed apiece, while No 252 Sqn's Flg Off Paul Nisbet, whose aircraft was damaged by return fire, and Sgt W Smith both fired on an S.79 that they believed was destroyed. Actually, only Capitano Marini's aircraft was shot down, with Mayer nursing his damaged torpedo-bomber back to base with wounded crewmen aboard. All of Marini's crew took to the dinghy except the flight engineer, 1° Aviere Motorista Giuseppe Colucci, who was never found. Luckily for the

Torpedo-bomber ace Tenente Giulio Cesare Graziani (far left) of 41° *Gruppo* briefs his 205ᵃ *Squadriglia* crew prior to taking off in early 1942. Second from left is Sergente Maggiore Giovanni Riso who flew as Graziani's co-pilot during several sorties throughout January and February 1942. He was badly wounded during the dramatic attack on a Tobruk-bound oiler on 5 February 1942 (*via author*)

five Italians, they were rescued that night by the German U-boat U-331, commanded by Kapitänleutnant Hans-Dietrich Frhr von Tiesenhausen, who had sunk *Barham*. The Italians spent six days aboard the U-boat before being disembarked in Piraeus harbour, Greece, on 22 February.

At 1600 hrs on 10 March two 205ᵃ *Squadriglia* S.79s (flown by Tenente Tourn and Sottotenente Mayer) attacked Rear Adm Philip Vian's Force 'B' (the cruisers *Naiad* and *Euryalus* and nine destroyers) to no avail – both S.79s returned damaged by naval fire. Vian's warships were targeted again at 1815 hrs by two more 205ᵃ *Squadriglia Sparvieri*, flown by 41° *Gruppo* CO Tenente Colonnello Ettore Muti and Sottotenente Cionni, again without success. Heavy anti-aircraft fire badly damaged Muti's trimotor. For this action Muti later received the Silver Medal for Military Valour.

On 13 March two 205ᵃ *Squadriglia* S.79s flown by Capitano Sondalini and Tenente Cristiani took off at 1120 hrs to attack a convoy off the Egyptian coast. They were intercepted by a pair of No 272 Sqn Beaufighters and two Hurricanes, probably from No 274 Sqn. Plt Off Derek Hammond of No 272 Sqn claimed a S.79 damaged off Tobruk, while the Italians claimed a Beaufighter shot down. Both S.79s, with torpedoes still attached, returned to base badly damaged at 1540 hrs.

SECOND BATTLE OF SIRTE

The disappointing outcome of Operation MF 5 from Alexandria in February, when three merchantmen, four cruisers and 16 destroyers attempted to reach Malta but were turned back by Axis aircraft without any supplies being delivered, forced Adm Cunningham to organise another supply convoy to Malta, codenamed MW 10. Thus the stage was set for the Second Battle of Sirte – the first engagement had taken place on 17 December 1941.

On 22 March the British convoy was attacked without effect in the morning by nine Libyan-based S.79s, five from 279ᵃ *Squadriglia* and four from 284ᵃ *Squadriglia*. During the first attack, at 0935 hrs, the 279ᵃ *Squadriglia* trimotors split into two formations, the fierce naval barrage forcing them to drop their torpedoes at long range. This action cost the life of Tenente Guglielmo Ranieri, killed with his crew by defensive fire from the warships, while Tenente Andrea Dell'Anna's S.79 had its tailplane badly damaged. The 284ᵃ *Squadriglia* aircraft attacked at 1107 hrs.

These were among the last actions flown by the two *squadriglie* as independent units, for on 25 March they jointly formed the new 131° *Gruppo Autonomo (Aut) AS*.

The Italians suffered further losses during an early evening attack at 1805 hrs on the 22nd. Six S.79s from 278ª *Squadriglia* and six from 130° *Gruppo's* 280ª and 283ª *Squadriglie* (three aircraft each) set off from the Sicilian airfield at Catania at around 1530 hrs. This time, amidst unconfirmed claims of hits and sinkings, three *Sparvieri* from 278ª *Squadriglia* were downed (one by naval ack-ack). They were flown by Sottotenenti Giovanni Scalia and Gaetano Marletta and Tenente Emilio Iuzzolino. The dramatic events of this mission were later recalled by Capitano Ugo Rivoli, CO of 278ª *Squadriglia*;

'While I aimed for the merchant ship, Scalia directed his aircraft against the warships, facing an infernal fire. Then we learned that, struck by anti-aircraft fire, he had managed to ditch in the vicinity of the Eolian Islands. The five crewmen settled in the raft which shortly afterwards was overwhelmed by a wave. Four died, but flight engineer Vito Bonfiglio saved himself as he returned to the aircraft to retrieve a compass. He was picked up the next day by a seaplane.

'A similar thing occurred with Marletta's crew. Forced to ditch off Cape Passero, having run out of fuel, Marletta, WO Albino Scalabrin and Flight Engineer Adriano Rossi disappeared forever after taking to the raft. Specialists Francesco Malara and Angelo Barba saved themselves because they remained aboard the aircraft, being picked up at 1000 hrs on 23 March by the torpedo boat *Stocco*.

'Iuzzolino met a dramatic end. Returning from the mission after attacking a merchantman, he crashed into a mountain in the locality of Roccella Jonica. None of the crew aboard was saved. To conclude, on 22 March 1942 the *squadriglia* of six aircraft lost three S.79s.'

The same action was also described by Tenente Francesco Aurelio Di Bella;

'Only six of us took off, because Capitano Frongia's aircraft was not airworthy. Aside from myself, the other 283ª *Squadriglia* pilots involved were Tenenti Roberto Cipriani and Francesco Cossu. The weather conditions, already poor when we took off from Elmas, soon worsened. We were really worried because we feared the mission would turn into a disaster due to the stormy seas. The High Command didn't share our point of view, insisting we had to attack. We were allowed one Ju 88 to lead us over the target.

'Immediately after takeoff, under the rain, we closed up our formation, flying at a height of just 50 m [160 ft]. We felt like we were on a roller coaster. After spotting the [battleship] *Littorio*, at 1800 hrs we discovered the British convoy. Melley and Setti attacked first, launching at a steamer. Then it was Greco's turn against an escort ship. Then Cipriani and me, aiming our torpedoes at a merchant ship.

S.79 278-11 flies low over a Sicilian beach near Catania in the spring of 1942. From 1 April that year the new 132° *Gruppo* was activated, comprising the formerly autonomous 278a and 281a *Squadriglie* (*Bundesarchiv*)

31

'Along with Cossu and Cipriani, we circled over the British ships to keep them engaged while they were under our fleet's large-calibre fire. As we were short of fuel we went to land at Benghazi. There, we were welcomed in a tent by Giulio Marini and Pulzetti, who had also returned from a second evening mission against the convoy, which was now no longer being tracked because of the darkness and mist.'

This action earned 'Ciccio' Di Bella his fourth Silver Medal for Military Valour. Between 23 and 27 March Convoy MW 10, delayed by the Italian fleet (which had damaged five of the escorting Allied warships), had four merchantmen sunk or disabled by German bombs.

The *Aerosiluranti*'s last sorties against the escort warships returning to Alexandria were made by 41° *Gruppo* on 23 and 24 March, all without result. The first action, at 1600 hrs on the 23rd, involved three S.79s led by Tenente Colonello Ettore Muti, whose aircraft (MM24302) was slightly damaged by anti-aircraft fire. The second sortie, by S.79s flown by Tenente Giorgio Tourn (205ª *Squadriglia*) and Sottotenente Antonio Monterumici (204ª *Squadriglia*), attacked at 0739 hrs on the 24th. Tourn's aircraft suffered an on-board fire during the return flight and he was forced to ditch. The crew took to their dinghy but were never found.

The British reported that the convoy had suffered 28 aerial attacks, with four enemy aircraft being claimed shot down by the cruiser HMS *Carlisle* and the destroyers.

At 1430 hrs on 30 March three 130° *Gruppo Sparvieri* (two from 280ª and one from 283ª *Squadriglie*) attacked a 7000-ton cruiser south of Galite Island. Although naval fire damaged the tailplane of Sottotenente Manlio Caresio's S.79 (280-5), he managed to drop his torpedo, which the cruiser avoided.

NEW *GRUPPI* FORMED

On 1 April the re-formed 281ª *Squadriglia*, led by Capitano Graziani, and 278ª *Squadriglia*, commanded by Capitano Rivoli, formed 132° *Gruppo Autonomo Aerosiluranti* (later based in Sicily between Castelvetrano and Gerbini). The new unit's CO was Capitano Buscaglia, who would soon prove to be a worthy leader.

The next significant action involving S.79 torpedo-bombers took place during the morning of 8 May when two 205ª *Squadriglia* aircraft (flown by Sottotenenti Emilio Pucci and Giuseppe Briatore, who took off at 0705 hrs) claimed hits on a freighter intercepted north of Kas Barum. After an uneventful dusk sortie the following day, five 280ª *Squadriglia* S.79s landed back at Pantelleria. Poor visibility over the airfield resulted in aircraft 280-5, flown by Tenente Renzo Sommadossi, crashing and bursting into flames, killing its crew. *Sparviero* 280-9, flown by Tenente Angelo Caponetti, also crashed, although only the flight engineer and gunner were injured.

This unidentified freighter was photographed on 8 May 1942 north of Kas Barum by two 205ª *Squadriglia Sparvieri* flown by Sottotenenti Emilio Pucci and Giuseppe Briatore. That morning the Italians claimed one torpedo hit apiece on the vessel – note the torpedo track highlighted by the arrow (*Aeronautica Militare*)

S.79 205-6 was the usual mount of 41° *Gruppo* torpedo-bomber ace Sottotenente Emilio Pucci di Barsento, the young Florentine nobleman accounting for the steamers *Stureborg* and *Aircrest*, which were both sunk in the eastern Mediterranean in June 1942. After the war Pucci distinguished himself again as an internationally renowned fashion designer (*Aeronautica Militare*)

On 11 May, after unsuccessfully attacking a steamer eight miles north of Port Said, two 204ª *Squadriglia* S.79s flown by Capitano De Stefano and Sottotenente Normanno White were intercepted by British fighters. Future ace Flg Off Michael Kinmonth in No 89 Sqn Beaufighter IF X7636 shot down White's *Sparviero*, which crashed north of Damietta, killing all of the crew. Kinmonth then turned his attention on De Stefano's S.79, which he damaged, killing one crewman and wounding two more.

Between December 1941 and May 1942 Italian torpedo-bombers, despite official claims, had not achieved a single torpedo hit. This incredible and awkward situation compelled *Generale di Squadra Aerea* Rino Corso Fougier (*Regia Aeronautica*'s Chief of Staff) to issue a series of official directives to *Aeronautica*'s commands and units to improve aircrews' combat effectiveness.

The torpedo-bombers' lack of success was at last relieved by the Aegean-based 41° *Gruppo* operating over in the Levant Sea. On 7 June two 204ª *Squadriglia Sparvieri* (MM24177, flown by Tenente Annona of 205ª *Squadriglia*, and MM24100, flown by Maresciallo Carrera) took off from Gadurra at 0605 hrs and intercepted an armed freighter and a gunboat off Port Said at 0940 hrs. Probably due to shallow soundings, Annona's torpedo missed the freighter. Seeing this, Carrera did not drop. But two days later, northeast of Alexandria, two S.79s of 204ª and 205ª *Squadriglie*, piloted by Tenente Luigi Vicariotto and Sottotenente Emilio Pucci, sank the 1661-ton Swedish steamer *Stureborg*.

Southwest of Jaffa at about 0800 hrs on 30 June an S.79 of 205ª *Squadriglia*, piloted by Sottotenente Emilio Pucci, sank the 5237-ton British steamer *Aircrest*. On 22 July the British 2980-ton rescue ship HMS *Malines* was torpedoed at 0920 hrs northeast of Port Said by two 205ª *Squadriglia* S.79s from Gadurra, these aircraft being flown by Sottotenenti Dorando Cionni and Ferruccio Coloni. The stricken ship reached Port Said, but it remained immobilised there until war's end.

A second torpedo-bomber unit formed on 1 April 1942, 133° *Gruppo* consisting of the already existing 174ª and 175ª *Squadriglie Ricognizione Strategica Terrestre* (land-based long-range reconnaissance squadrons). 133° Gruppo's two sub-units were initially based at Benghazi K2 (174ª *Squadriglia*) and Castel Benito (175ª *Squadriglia*) airfields in Libya. In accordance with the Libyan theatre's requirements, these *squadriglie* flew mainly naval convoy escorts and attack-reconnaissance sorties, rarely being employed in the torpedo-bomber role. Effectiveness in the latter role was achieved by 20 September, but the unit's non-torpedo-bomber tasking in 1942 proved to be just as dangerous.

On 4 June Tenente De Michelis, flying in a convoy-escorting 174ª *Squadriglia* S.79, intercepted and fired on a Beaufighter, but he broke off the pursuit when his forward machine gun jammed. Eleven days later a 174ª *Squadriglia* shadower flown by (*text continues on page 46*)

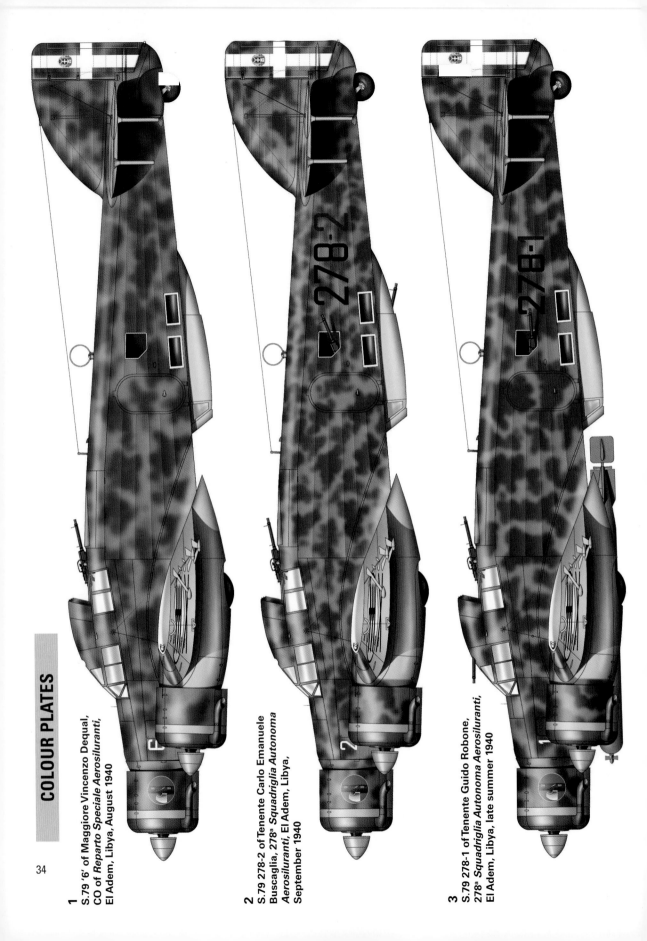

COLOUR PLATES

1
S.79 '6' of Maggiore Vincenzo Dequal,
CO of *Reparto Speciale Aerosiluranti*,
El Adem, Libya, August 1940

2
S.79 278-2 of Tenente Carlo Emanuele
Buscaglia, 278ª *Squadriglia Autonoma
Aerosiluranti*, El Adem, Libya,
September 1940

3
S.79 278-1 of Tenente Guido Robone,
278ª *Squadriglia Autonoma Aerosiluranti*,
El Adem, Libya, late summer 1940

34

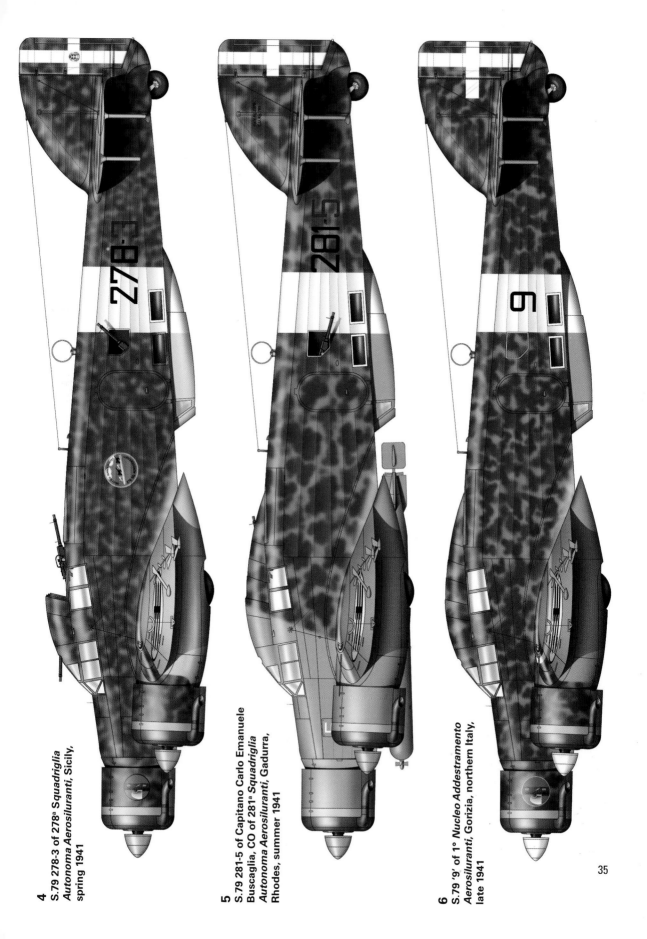

4
S.79 278-3 of 278ª *Squadriglia Autonoma Aerosiluranti*, Sicily, spring 1941

5
S.79 281-5 of Capitano Carlo Emanuele Buscaglia, CO of 281ª *Squadriglia Autonoma Aerosiluranti*, Gadurra, Rhodes, summer 1941

6
S.79 '9' of 1° *Nucleo Addestramento Aerosiluranti*, Gorizia, northern Italy, late 1941

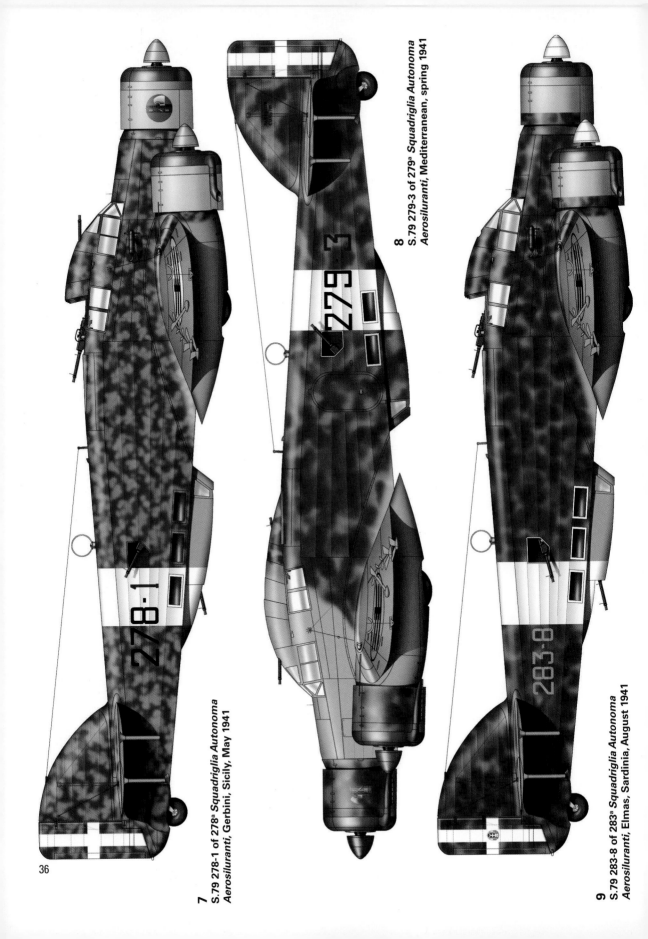

36

7
S.79 278-1 of 278ª *Squadriglia Autonoma Aerosiluranti*, Gerbini, Sicily, May 1941

8
S.79 279-3 of 279ª *Squadriglia Autonoma Aerosiluranti*, Mediterranean, spring 1941

9
S.79 283-8 of 283ª *Squadriglia Autonoma Aerosiluranti*, Elmas, Sardinia, August 1941

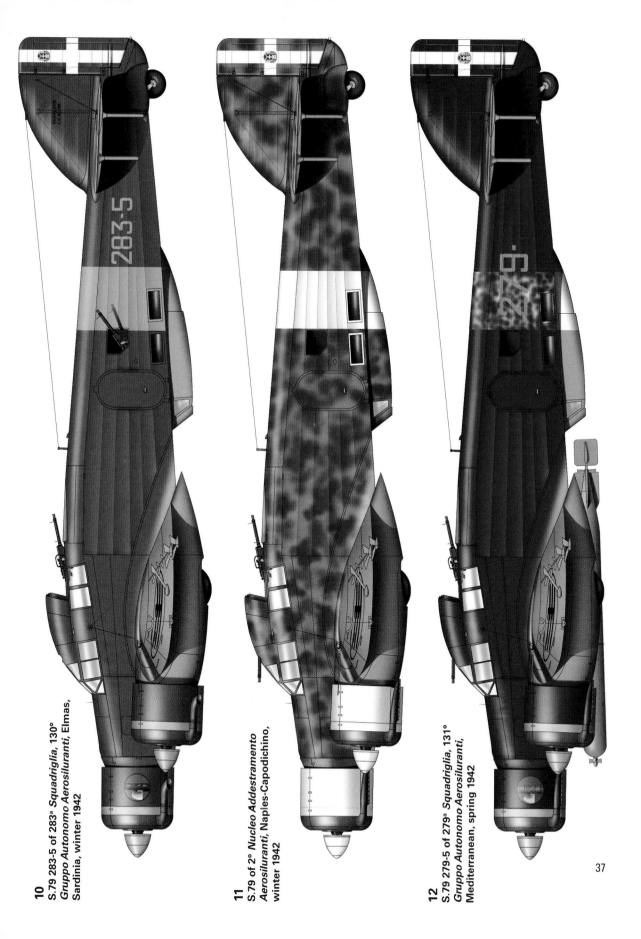

10
S.79 283-5 of 283ª *Squadriglia*, 130°
Gruppo Autonomo Aerosiluranti, Elmas,
Sardinia, winter 1942

11
S.79 of 2° *Nucleo Addestramento
Aerosiluranti*, Naples-Capodichino,
winter 1942

12
S.79 279-5 of 279ª *Squadriglia*, 131°
Gruppo Autonomo Aerosiluranti,
Mediterranean, spring 1942

37

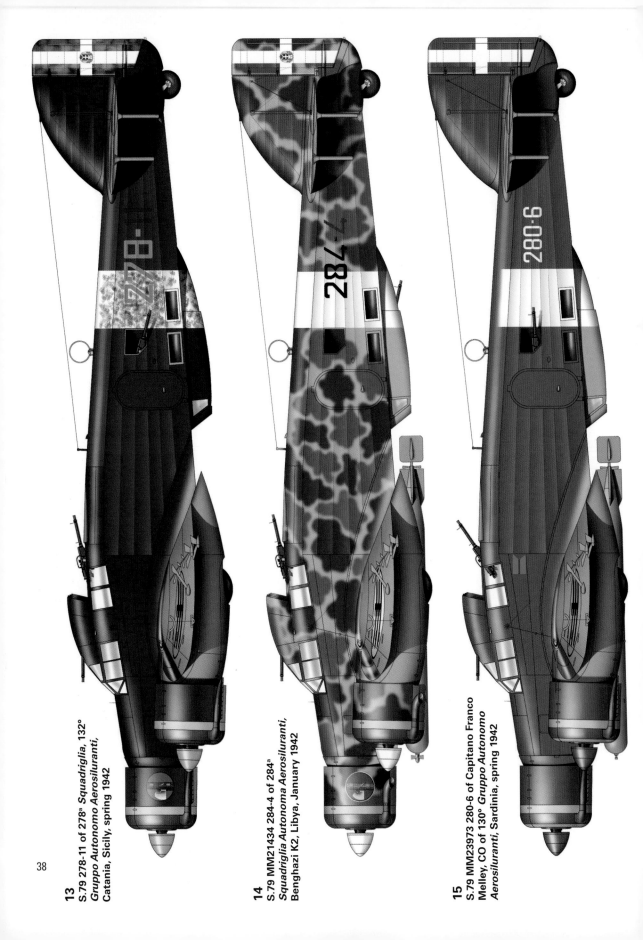

13
S.79 278-11 of 278ª *Squadriglia*, 132°
Gruppo Autonomo Aerosiluranti,
Catania, Sicily, spring 1942

14
S.79 MM21434 284-4 of 284ª
Squadriglia Autonoma Aerosiluranti,
Benghazi K2, Libya, January 1942

15
S.79 MM23973 280-6 of Capitano Franco
Melley, CO of 130° *Gruppo Autonomo
Aerosiluranti,* Sardinia, spring 1942

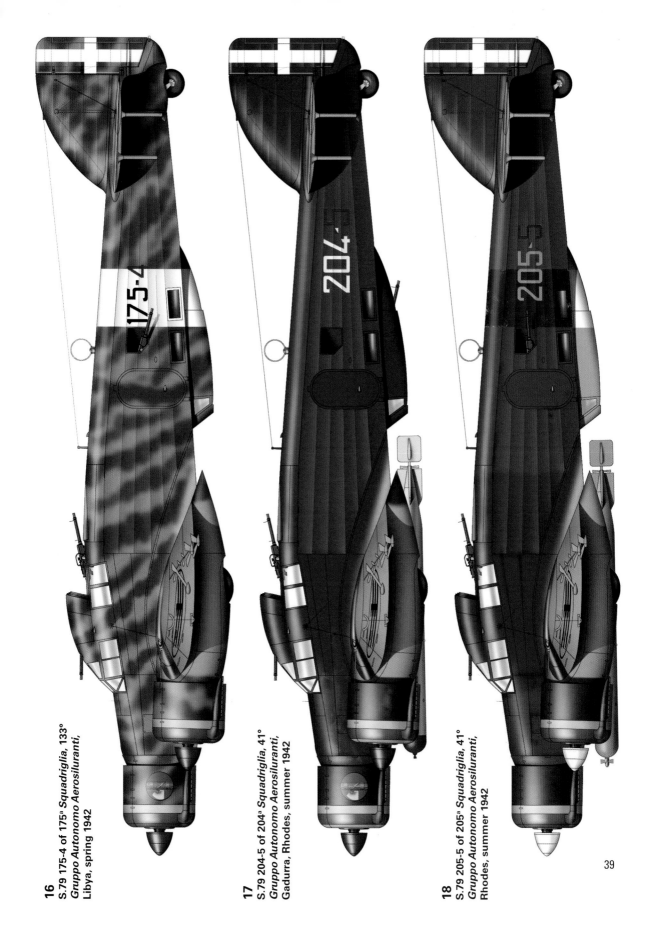

16
S.79 175-4 of 175ª *Squadriglia*, 133°
Gruppo Autonomo Aerosiluranti,
Libya, spring 1942

17
S.79 204-5 of 204ª *Squadriglia*, 41°
Gruppo Autonomo Aerosiluranti,
Gadurra, Rhodes, summer 1942

18
S.79 205-5 of 205ª *Squadriglia*, 41°
Gruppo Autonomo Aerosiluranti,
Rhodes, summer 1942

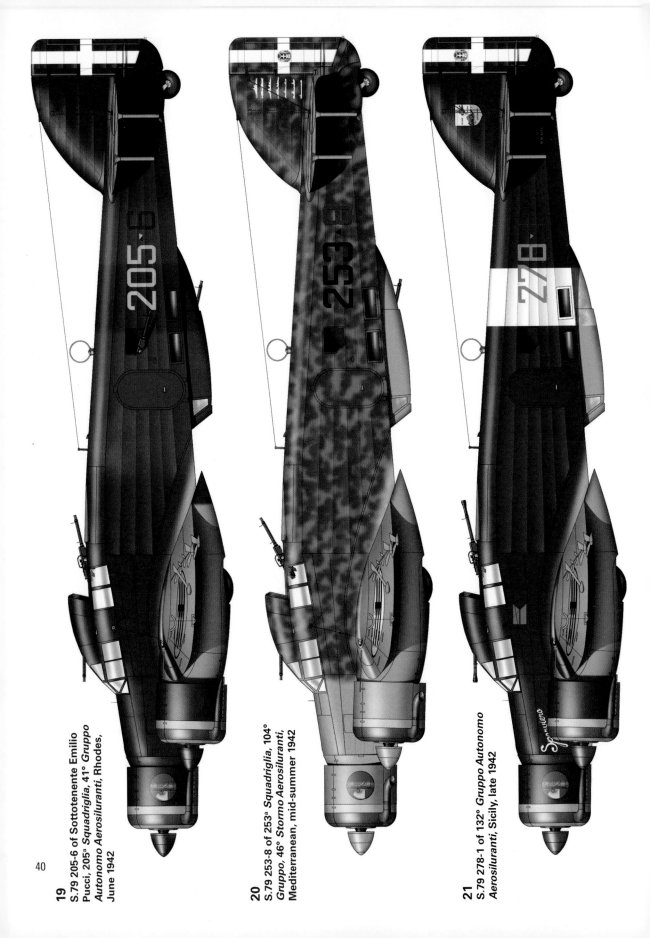

40

19
S.79 205-6 of Sottotenente Emilio
Pucci, 205ª *Squadriglia, 41° Gruppo
Autonomo Aerosiluranti*, Rhodes,
June 1942

20
S.79 253-8 of 253ª *Squadriglia, 104°
Gruppo, 46° Stormo Aerosiluranti*,
Mediterranean, mid-summer 1942

21
S.79 278-1 of 132° *Gruppo Autonomo
Aerosiluranti*, Sicily, late 1942

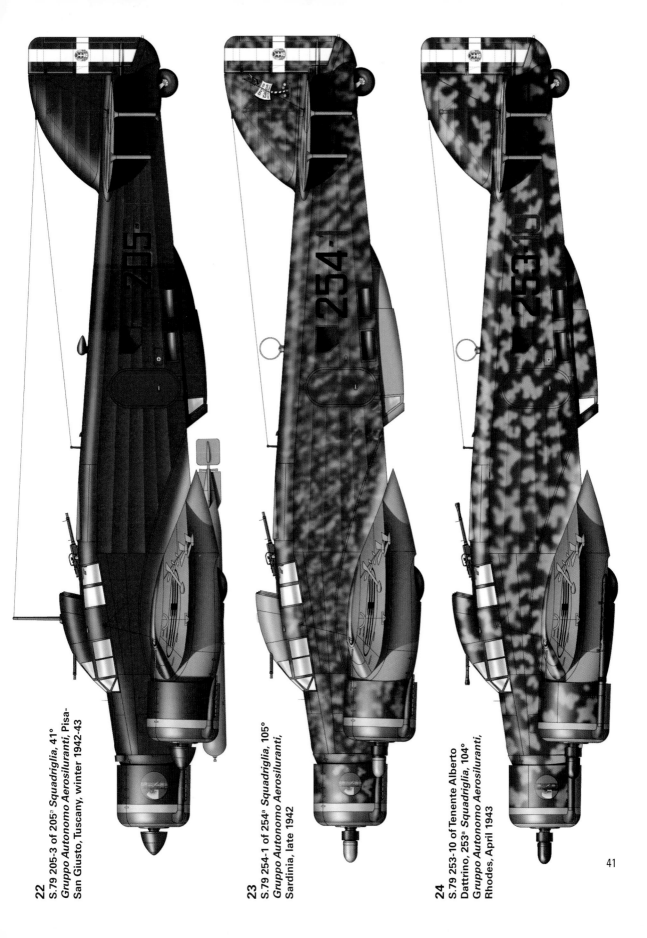

22
S.79 205-3 of 205ª *Squadriglia, 41°
Gruppo Autonomo Aerosiluranti*, Pisa-
San Giusto, Tuscany, winter 1942-43

23
S.79 254-1 of 254ª *Squadriglia, 105°
Gruppo Autonomo Aerosiluranti*,
Sardinia, late 1942

24
S.79 253-10 of Tenente Alberto
Dattrino, 253ª *Squadriglia, 104°
Gruppo Autonomo Aerosiluranti*,
Rhodes, April 1943

41

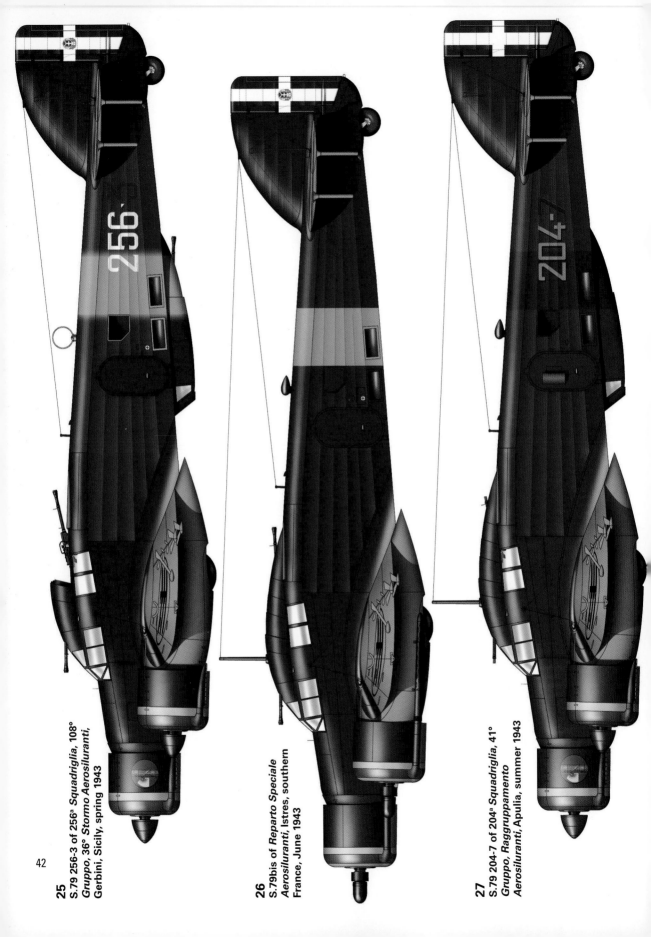

25
S.79 256-3 of 256ª *Squadriglia*, 108°
Gruppo, 36° Stormo Aerosiluranti,
Gerbini, Sicily, spring 1943

26
S.79bis of *Reparto Speciale
Aerosiluranti*, Istres, southern
France, June 1943

27
S.79 204-7 of 204ª *Squadriglia*, 41°
*Gruppo, Raggruppamento
Aerosiluranti*, Apulia, summer 1943

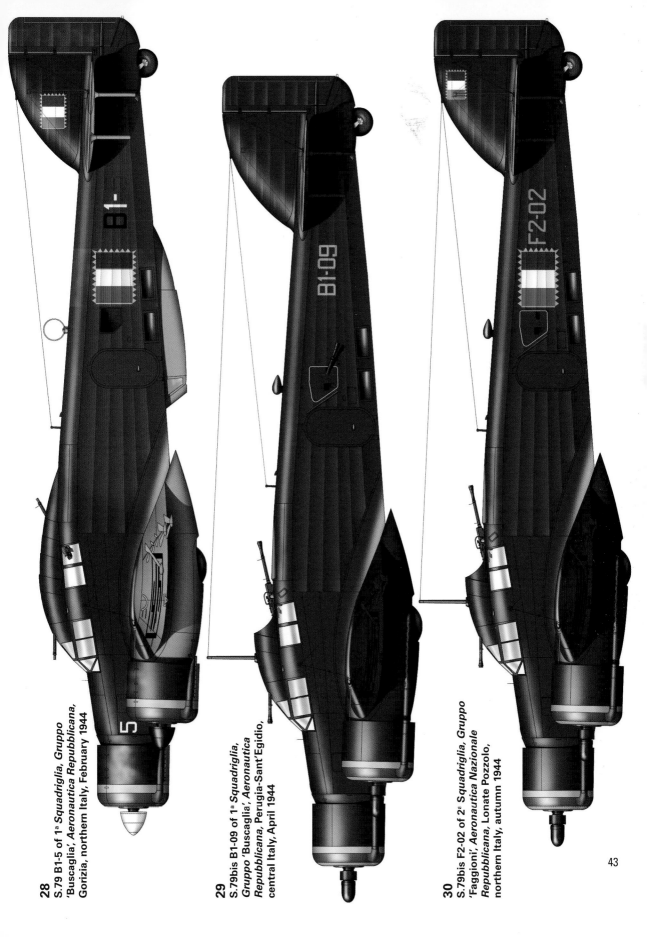

28
S.79 B1-5 of 1ª Squadriglia, Gruppo 'Buscaglia', Aeronautica Repubblicana, Gorizia, northern Italy, February 1944

29
S.79bis B1-09 of 1ª Squadriglia, Gruppo 'Buscaglia', Aeronautica Repubblicana, Perugia-Sant'Egidio, central Italy, April 1944

30
S.79bis F2-02 of 2ª Squadriglia, Gruppo 'Faggioni', Aeronautica Nazionale Repubblicana, Lonate Pozzolo, northern Italy, autumn 1944

43

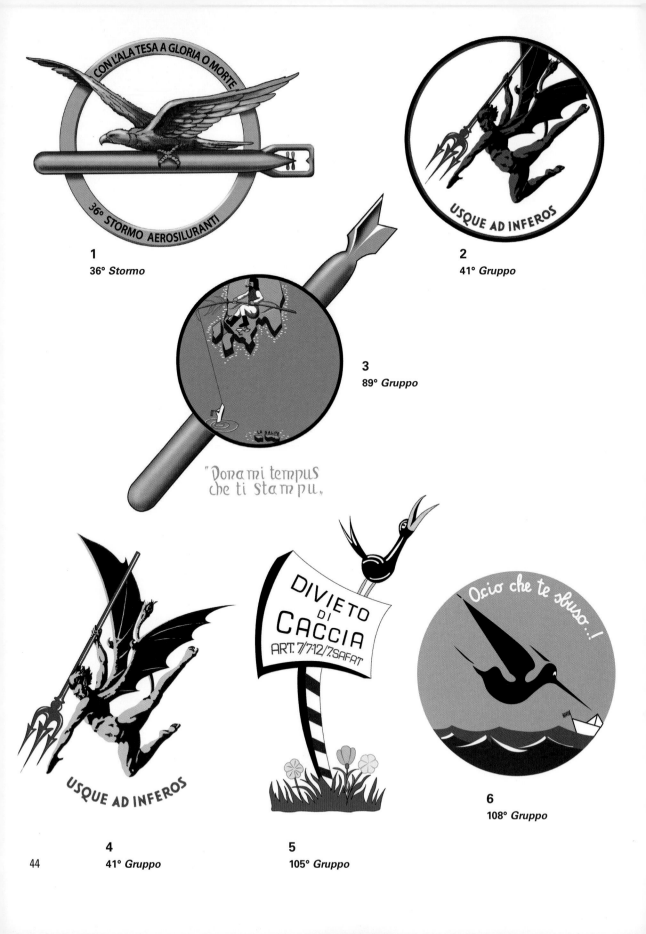

1
36° *Stormo*

2
41° *Gruppo*

3
89° *Gruppo*

"Donami tempus che ti stampu"

4
41° *Gruppo*

5
105° *Gruppo*

6
108° *Gruppo*

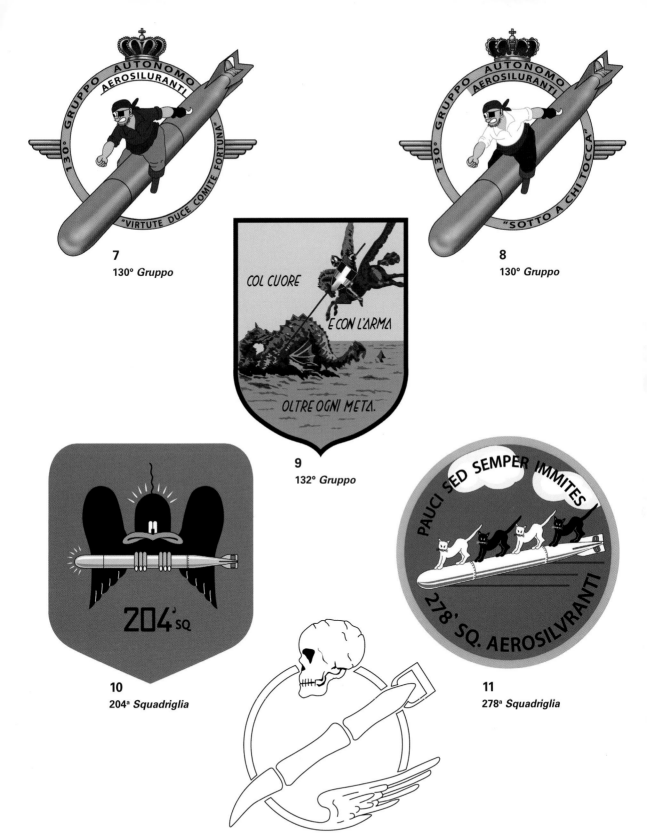

7
130° *Gruppo*

8
130° *Gruppo*

9
132° *Gruppo*

10
204ª *Squadriglia*

11
278ª *Squadriglia*

12
279ª *Squadriglia*

45

Tenente Micci, searching for the British Convoy *Vigorous*, was attacked by a No 272 Sqn Beaufighter flown by Plt Off Noel Cleggett, who damaged the S.79's starboard engine. The *Sparviero* returned to base on two engines after a 248-mile flight.

Through the second half of September 133° *Gruppo*'s 174ª *Squadriglia* strafed trucks of the Long Range Desert Group (LRDG) that were attacking the Jalo Oasis. During the afternoon of the 15th four S.79s strafed ten trucks near Wadi Belgardan and set seven aflame, one S.79 being hit by ground fire. The next day two *Sparvieri* took off at 0845 hrs and bombed and set ablaze three vehicles 100 km (60 miles) southwest of Jalo. During their return flight, at 1200 hrs, the S.79s strafed R2 patrol's Chevrolet trucks, led by Lt Talbot. The LRDG men returned fire fiercely, badly damaging an S.79 and wounding three airmen. That same afternoon another *Sparviero* strafed vehicles hiding in the northwestern corner of the Jalo Oasis, claiming three set alight.

On the morning of 17 September two S.79s bombed the Jalo Oasis's northwestern sector. That afternoon another two S.79s attacked the same target, Tenente Nicoletti boldly strafing at low level. The following day three S.79s strafed and bombed the oasis again, one trimotor being seriously hit by ground fire. An S.79 trio raided Jalo again on the 19th, claiming three trucks effectively strafed. On the 22nd the LRDG's logistic depot was discovered by Tenente Baroni's S.79, which strafed some vehicles. The next day the Italians freed the besieged oasis, the LRDG being forced to retreat.

On 6 October two 174ª *Squadriglia* S.79s flown by Sottotenente Sponza and Sergente Canis collided on takeoff, sustaining damage. Nine days later another *Sparviero* from the same unit, flown by Sottotenente Galluzzi and escorting a naval convoy, spotted a submarine periscope 23 miles north of Homs and dropped two bombs on it.

On 14 November S.79 MM21812 of 174ª *Squadriglia*, flown by Tenente Nicoletti, was bounced by nine British fighters near Agedabia. The S.79 had one engine hit, but its crew escaped unhurt, the pilot later being awarded the Silver Medal for Military Valour.

Towards the end of November 133° *Gruppo* personnel began their repatriation to Libya, the unit finally being disbanded on the last day of 1942.

LAUNCHING AT THE CARRIER *ARGUS*

At 1900 hrs on 18 May 1942 three 130° *Gruppo Sparvieri* took off from Sardinian Elmas airport. Flying S.79 280-6, Capitano Franco Melley led two others (one each from 280ª and 283ª *Squadriglie*) in an attack on the carrier HMS *Argus*, escorted by the cruiser HMS *Charybdis* and seven destroyers. Along with the carrier HMS *Eagle*, *Argus* was involved in Operation LB, which had seen *Eagle* launch 17 Spitfires and six Albacore biplanes as reinforcements for Malta. After the last Spitfire had left the flightdeck, the Albacores took off just before sunset on the 18th, whereupon the carriers and their escorts turned back westwards. However, two hours later the six biplanes landed back onboard *Eagle* after their engines began to overheat

At 2110 hrs, west-southwest of Sardinia between the island and the Algerian coast, the three Italian aircraft spotted the British warships. The vessels opened fire at 2135 hrs, hitting the 283ª *Squadriglia* S.79

The steamer *Tanimbar* blows up on 14 June 1942 after being torpedoed by a 104° *Gruppo* aircraft and finished off by 9° *Stormo* Z.1007bis level bombers (*Aeronautica Militare*)

British naval fire seriously damaged this S.79 flown by 253ª *Squadriglia* CO Capitano Solimena and 104° *Gruppo* CO Maggiore Virginio Reinero during the attack on the *Harpoon* convoy. The aircraft, credited with hitting the steamer *Tanimbar* with a torpedo, made it back to base despite the damage (*Aeronautica Militare*)

flown by Tenente Camillo Barioglio. After releasing his torpedo, Barioglio was forced to ditch 40 miles north of Cape Bengut (in Algeria), two crewmembers being seriously injured. After spending 20 hours in their dinghy Barioglio's crew was picked up by an Italian rescue aircraft.

Melley followed Barioglio in his attack on the ships, flying his S.79 through the vessels' defensive fire and closing in on *Argus* before dropping his torpedo. The Italians stated that the weapon drop was followed 'by a formidable explosion close by', which made them think that the carrier had been hit. Meanwhile, Melley's port wingman, Sottotenente Manlio Caresio (in S.79 280-2), had attacked *Charybdis*. The war diary of 130° *Gruppo* states that the cruiser was hit and forced to reduce speed. However, British reports note that the convoy was unsuccessfully attacked by torpedo-bombers at 2200 hrs. The Italian torpedoes had missed. The S.79s had endured a fierce anti-aircraft barrage during their daring attacks, the 130° *Gruppo* war diary stating, 'Now the enraged bursts from the machine guns of the enemy units tried to hit the aircraft'. Nevertheless, Melley and Caresio landed safely at Elmas at 2350 hrs.

Targeting Malta-bound convoys continued in June, when the *Sparvieri* forces from Sardinia and Sicily were heavily engaged attacking ships from Convoys *Harpoon* and *Vigorous*. The Italians called these operations the 'Battle of Mid-June'. To prevent Axis air forces engaging the convoys, Allied desert raiding parties attacked aircraft in their 'nests'. On 13 June a Free French Special Air Service (SAS) patrol led by Lt André Zirnheld attacked Berka airfield, but it was repelled by armed sentries. One French raider was captured and just three 284ª *Squadriglia* (131° *Gruppo*) S.79s were slightly damaged by bullets.

On 14 June the first aircraft airborne to attack *Harpoon* were 36° *Stormo*'s only two S.79s, which led eight 24° *Gruppo* CR.42 fighter-bombers against the convoy. During this raid two Sea Hurricanes of 801 NAS, flown by Lt F R A Turnbull and Sub Lt Duthie, destroyed a *Sparviero* of 259ª *Squadriglia* (109° *Gruppo*) flown by Tenente Alberto Leonardi. There were no survivors. A second much larger force was sent aloft from Sardinia at 0900 hrs, the *Aerosiluranti* contribution comprising nine 130° and ten 104° *Gruppi* S.79s and fifteen 36° *Stormo* S.84s. Once they had spotted the convoy at around 1000 hrs, the Italians split into two formations, one attacking vessels in the port column and the other sweeping along the starboard side. The starboard attackers were the ten 104° and eight (one had aborted) 130° *Gruppi* S.79s.

104° *Gruppo*'s aircraft attacked at 1007 hrs, and during their action the 8169-ton Dutch steamer *Tanimbar* was struck by a torpedo, probably dropped by *gruppo* CO Maggiore Virginio Reinero, whose 253ᵃ *Squadriglia* S.79 was damaged by anti-aircraft fire. Later, 18 9° *Stormo* Z.1007bis trimotors attacked from the port side, bombing and finishing off *Tanimbar* and killing 23 of those onboard.

In this hard-fought action 104° *Gruppo* lost two 253ᵃ *Squadriglia* S.79s flown by Tenente Giovanni Vivarelli Colonna and Tenente Mario Ingrellini. Both crews perished. Ten Colonna's S.79 was shot down by an 807 NAS Fulmar, he and his crew being awarded the posthumous Silver Medal and Bronze Medals for Military Valour, respectively. Ingrellini's aircraft fell to anti-aircraft fire. Two more 253ᵃ *Squadriglia Sparvieri*, flown by Tenenti Enrico Marescalchi and Eugenio Taverna, were damaged, Marescalchi's badly. It crash-landed wheels-up near Cape Teulada, in Sardinia.

In this action 807 NAS lost Sub Lt Peter Palmer and Lt Philip Hall (both killed), who had shared in the destruction of two S.79s. 801 NAS's CO, ace Lt Cdr Rupert Brabner, was credited with an S.79 destroyed and another as a probable near Sardinia, while squadronmate Sub Lt Godfrey Parish claimed an S.79 as badly damaged – his Sea Hurricane was hit by its return fire.

The 104° *Gruppo* losses on 14 June testified to the great courage displayed by Tenente Ingrellini's aircrew. Born in Lucca in 1915, Mario Ingrellini was already a veteran, having been decorated with the Bronze Medal for Military Valour for actions on both the French and Greek-Albanian fronts. His co-pilot, Sergente Maggiore Giorgio Compiani, born in Parma in 1915, was a veteran of the Spanish Civil War. He shared Ingrellini's high sense of duty and love of his country, and passion for the torpedo-bomber mission. Both men were able to instil their crewmen with their fervour for victory, teaching them to be bold but not reckless, facing risks coolly and quietly.

Before taking off to attack the *Harpoon* ships, Ingrellini and Compiani were determined to torpedo a British carrier. As if having a premonition, Compiani wrote to his CO, his friends and his parents, informing all of them of his deep feelings. While calmly awaiting the order to take off, Ingrellini declared without boasting and with serenity that he was determined to hit the carrier, even if it cost him his life. To underline his determination he wrote the ship's name with his fingertip in the grease covering the warhead of his torpedo. Ingrellini then summoned his crew and, with Compiani's support, imbued them with the same will of victory, while not making light of the dangers.

Once the Italian aircraft reached the convoy, the S.79 crews following

Tenente Enrico Marescalchi's crew appear to be very relieved after their escape from danger. Their damaged 253ᵃ *Squadriglia* S.79 crash-landed in Sardinia on 14 June 1942 after attacking the *Harpoon* convoy. They are, from left to right, flight engineer Aviere Scelto Ottavio Grigolon, wireless operator 1° Aviere Luciano Vernier, gunner Aviere Scelto Guerrino Ferretti, pilot Tenente Marescalchi and co-pilot Sergente Eugenio Guerrini *(Courtesy Andrea Marescalchi)*

On 14 June 1942 Tenente Mario Ingrellini perished along with his crew while attacking the carrier HMS *Eagle*. His determination earned him a posthumous *Medaglia d'Oro al Valor Militare* (*Aeronautica Militare*)

Ingrellini's and Compiani as they ignored two easy targets whilst boldly threading their way between a battleship and a cruiser screening the carrier *Eagle*. Although their S.79 had already been hit, they aimed at the carrier and dropped their torpedo. As Ingrellini tried to disengage, his aircraft was struck again in one engine and in the wing, and the latter started to burn. The *Sparviero* was probably hit by *Eagle*'s anti-aircraft batteries, as these claimed to have downed an S.79 that had launched a torpedo at the carrier from an altitude of just 36 m (120 ft) and at a range of 366 m (400 yds), without success.

Realising their S.79 was doomed, the Italians tried to crash into an enemy ship. The *Sparviero*, its wing aflame, left the centre of the convoy and shortly thereafter was seen seeking a target among the vessels. However, it suddenly crashed at speed into the sea in a ball of fire. During the action the gun crews of the destroyer HMS *Icarus* and the carrier *Argus* claimed an S.79 shot down apiece, so the destruction of Ingrellini's *Sparviero* should be credited to one or both of these ships.

For the courage displayed in this attack, Tenente Mario Ingrellini and Sergente Maggiore Giorgio Compiani were both posthumously awarded the Gold Medal for Military Valour. The other crewmen, 1° Aviere Armiere (gunner) Valentini and Avieri Scelti Pirro (flight engineer) and Bazzicchi (wireless operator) were posthumously awarded the Silver Medal for Military Valour.

Meanwhile, the eight 130° *Gruppo* S.79s (four each from 280ª and 283ª *Squadriglie*) had also attacked, the formation splitting up in two four-strong wedge-shaped patrols flying side by side. The convoy put up fierce anti-aircraft fire, hitting all of the Italian aircraft. The cruiser HMS *Liverpool* was the main target of four 280ª *Squadriglia* S.79s flown by Capitano Franco Melley (280-12), Tenenti Alessandro Setti (280-1) and Angelo Caponetti (280-5) and Sottotenente Manlio Caresio (280-2). Their torpedoes were released from 30 m (100 ft) at a range of 1830 m (2000 yds). Two weapons crossed the cruiser's bow and passed down its port side and another passed under the stern, but the fourth torpedo struck *Liverpool* aft on the starboard side. Fifteen of the ship's crew were killed and 22 injured. After their successful attack, 130° *Gruppo*'s S.79s disengaged and returned to their Sardinian base at 1150 hrs. Another source credits *Liverpool*'s hit to 104° *Gruppo*'s 252° *Squadriglia*.

At 1145 hrs the crippled cruiser turned back to Gibraltar, later being taken in tow by the destroyer HMS *Antelope* and escorted by the destroyer HMS *Westcott*. These ships duly attracted the attention of Sardinian-based aircraft at 1745 hrs, when three 104° and five 130° *Gruppi Sparvieri* (two from 283ª and three from 280ª *Squadriglie*), led by Tenente Angelo Caponetti in 280-5 and escorted by 14 24° *Gruppo* CR.42s, attacked. All of the torpedoes missed, and fierce anti-aircraft fire downed the 253ª *Squadriglia* S.79 flown by Tenente Giovanni Giacomello. The crew took to their dinghy and were captured the next morning by the destroyer HMS *Vidette*.

Liverpool was attacked again that evening by three 3° *Nucleo AS Sparvieri*, but the cruiser easily avoided all of their torpedoes. The last attack on the cruiser and its escorts, made by three 2° *Nucleo AS* S.79s, came late in the morning of 15 June. The Italians were intercepted by two 801 NAS Hurricanes, again flown by Lt 'Dick' Turnbull and Sub Lt 'Red' Duthie, who concentrated their attacks on the S.79 piloted by Tenente Lelio Silva.

With its starboard engine in flames, it plunged into the sea, killing the crew. Tenente Silva posthumously received the Gold Medal for Military Valour.

Liverpool, now towed by the tug HMS *Salvonia,* which had relieved *Antelope,* reached Gibraltar on the afternoon of the 17th and then underwent repairs in dry dock.

During the late afternoon of 14 June 14 S.79s (seven each from 278ª and 281ª *Squadriglie*) of 132° *Gruppo,* led by Capitano Buscaglia, took off from Sicily at 1745 hrs and attacked the British ships northwest of Cape Blanc. En route they were intercepted by two Sea Hurricanes of 801 NAS, again piloted by Turnbull and Duthie, who struck hard. The S.79 of Sottotenente Giannino Negri of 278ª *Squadriglia* was downed, killing all onboard, and the *Sparviero* of Sottotenente Vittorio Moretti was so badly damaged that the pilot had to crash-land at Castelvetrano, in Sicily, with three crewmen wounded. The remaining 132° *Gruppo Sparvieri* were all hit by naval fire, wounding a further two crewmen. The S.79s' gunners returned fire, riddling Lt Turnbull's fuel tank with bullets – he barely made it back to *Eagle.*

During the action four S.79s targeted *Argus,* among them Tenenti Faggioni and Graziani, both of whom made low-level attacks on the carrier. An S.79 'probable' was claimed by ace Sub Lt Mike Crosley in a Sea Hurricane of 813 NAS.

The next day saw three *Sparvieri* flown by Capitano Buscaglia, Tenente Umberto Camera and Sottotenente Martino Aichner clash with a No 235 Sqn Beaufighter, which damaged all three S.79s. Tenente Camera's aircraft was badly damaged and three crewmen wounded, the aircraft being forced to land on Pantelleria Island. Camera later provided an account of the episode;

'On Monday morning [15 June], torpedoes loaded, we set off again in search of the ships. After about an hour a Beaufighter attacked us. I was, as usual, the right wingman of Capitano Buscaglia. The British fighter pilot attacked from the right, hitting my aircraft with his first burst. Three crew were wounded and a fire started aboard. Nevertheless, my gunners continued shooting as though nothing had happened. The wireless operator was at the upper machine gun and the photographer and the gunner manned the waist ones, while the flight engineer, unable to use the damaged fire extinguisher, didn't hesitate to extinguish the fire, which had spread to the auxiliary tank (luckily empty!), with the flying suit he wore.

'In a few moments all on board was normal again and, while I was busy maintaining a patrol with the formation leader, my crew repelled two more attacks by the Beaufighter pilot, who, probably seeing my aircraft smoking, seemed sure of forcing me to take an involuntary bath.

'I felt ferocious rage because I could not return the enemy's fire, though I wanted to shoot him down at any cost, and bitter resignation when I saw the fire on board which, if it had not been extinguished

Tenente Lelio Silva of 2° *Nucleo AS* was shot down and killed along with his crew by two 801 NAS Sea Hurricanes on 15 June 1942 during one of the fruitless Italian attacks aimed at finishing off the damaged cruiser HMS *Liverpool* (*Aeronautica Militare*)

An S.79 gunner is ready for action behind his 7.7 mm Breda-SAFAT machine gun during a sortie in 1942. This weapon was both reliable and fast-firing (900 rounds per minute), although there was only sufficient room in the fuselage for one man to operate both fuselage-mounted 7.7 mm guns (*Aeronautica Militare*)

immediately, would have compelled me to ditch. However, everything went well until we landed on Pantelleria. The numerous hits had shredded the starboard undercarriage and, while I was taxiing in, pleased with my really smooth landing, I suddenly found the machine on its belly owing to a collapsed wheel. You can imagine my rage at seeing the aircraft irretrievably damaged. I was

This action photograph shows Capitano Buscaglia's *Sparviero* running in to attack the battleship HMS *Malaya* and the carrier HMS *Argus* in the late afternoon of 14 June 1942 (*Aeronautica Militare*)

deprived of another magnificent torpedo-bombing action, in which Sottotenente Aichner and Capitano Buscaglia had also been protagonists. But I will get my revenge next time!'

Camera was subsequently promoted to capitano and posted to 229ª *Squadriglia*, 89° *Gruppo*, equipped with S.84 torpedo-bombers. He was killed in combat with Spitfires of No 81 Sqn during an attack on Allied shipping in Bone Harbour on 1 December 1942.

After their S.79s had been repaired, Buscaglia and Aichner took off again. At about 1330 hrs Buscaglia spotted the stationary steamer *Burdwan*, which had already been bombed by I./KG 54's Ju 88s, and launched his torpedo at it. Some sources credit its sinking to the Italian torpedo ace, but it is worth noting that, according to Generale Graziani's evidence, the bewildered Buscaglia did not see the weapon's track after it hit the water. In fact, the 132° *Gruppo* war diary reports only the torpedo launch, without mentioning a hit. Buscaglia's weapon probably sank just after touching the water, as instances of sabotage were later discovered at the Neapolitan Baia torpedo factory. The doomed *Burdwan,* after being bombed by KüFlGr 606's Ju 88s as well, finally sank at 1420 hrs, its end being witnessed from Italian 7th Division warships.

Meanwhile, S.79 MM23942, flown by Sottotenente Aichner, attacked the British destroyer HMS *Bedouin*, which had been immobilised by gunfire from Italian cruisers of the 7th Division. Aichner's torpedo hit the destroyer, but before it sank with the loss of 28 men it shot down the *Sparviero*. Aichner and his crew took to their life raft and were saved by an Italian rescue seaplane. Later, Aichner recalled the *Bedouin* attack;

'On the morning of the 15th three of us – Buscaglia, Camera and

The British destroyer HMS *Bedouin* sinks on 15 June 1942 after being torpedoed near Pantelleria by a 132° *Gruppo* S.79 flown by Sottotenente Martino Aichner (*Aeronautica Militare*)

myself – took off with the last torpedoes at our disposal, but a British fighter attacked us and we were forced to land on Pantelleria. Camera's S.79 was in bad shape. Two of us remained, but one of my engines refused to start. The flight engineer got busy, but Buscaglia was in a hurry and took off, escorted by some fighters. At last I too restarted, with the vain hope of catching the commander. The order was to attack the convoy's cargo ships and let the warships go, but the ones I spotted had been struck and their fate sealed. I headed back for two destroyers previously spotted, with one proceeding under tow – it had been hit by cruisers from our 7th Division. Now, the vessel was alone and progressing slowly.

'I lined up for an attack and dived, but the ship fired, using all of its weapons. I dropped at about 600 m [650 yds] range, and almost at the same time they hit one of my engines. I was too close, unable to make an evasive turn. I could only pass over the British ship, and I took more strikes. I was forced to ditch two miles away from my victim. At about 1300 hrs we took to the life raft, all six of us unharmed. Shortly after *Bedouin* went to the bottom. Towards 2000 hrs we were picked up by one of our rescue seaplanes.'

For propaganda purposes the Italian authorities initially credited *Bedouin*'s loss to the Italian Navy, rather than to Aichner. Nevertheless, for this action he was awarded the Silver Medal for Military Valour. Only in April 1988, after accurate joint Italian and British research, was this sinking credited to Aichner, earning him the *Medaglia d'Oro al Valor Militare*.

The actions of 15 June did not end there, however. That afternoon the British Convoy *Vigorous*, sailing from the Levant, was attacked by ten Italian torpedo-bombers. Six of these, from 279ª *Squadriglia* of 131° *Gruppo*, had taken off from Cyrenaica, while the remaining four from 204ª *Squadriglia* (one was flown by a 205ª *Squadriglia* crew) of 41° *Gruppo* got airborne from Rhodes. According to Capitano Marini's post-war statement, reported in the 279ª *Squadriglia* war diary, five 284ª *Squadriglia* (also from 131° *Gruppo*) S.79s took part in this action as well. Thus, the *Sparvieri* attackers initially numbered 15, but they were later reduced to 14 when Sottotenente Romeo Mutti of 279ª *Squadriglia* aborted the mission at 1545 hrs.

The 131° *Gruppo* S.79s attacked between 1710 hrs and 1735 hrs and the 41° *Gruppo* aircraft did so at 1725 hrs. They tried to strike the convoy from both sides, but the British ships avoided all of their torpedoes by rapid manoeuvring. One S.79 of 41° *Gruppo*, flown by Tenente Salvatore Annona of 205ª *Squadriglia*, was shot down by No 252 Sqn Beaufighter T4831 flown by Plt Off Easton Thwaites as part of the convoy's air cover. All of the crew were killed. Kittyhawk-equipped No 250 Sqn, which was also providing fighter cover, claimed some S.79s too – Plt Off Percy Copeland, in AK955/'A', was credited with two destroyed and Sgt F C De Salvo Hall claimed

Sottotenente Martino Aichner's crew who sank the destroyer *Bedouin*. These men are, from left to right, Avieri Scelti Mario Picerno and Massimiliano Fantuzzi, co-pilot Sergente Maggiore Oreste Del Buono, Sottotenente Martino Aichner and Avieri Mario De Santis and Carmine Pragliola (*via author*)

Torpedo-bomber crews possibly from 204ª, 41° *Gruppo AS* pose in 'summer dress' in Rhodes in mid 1942 (*via author*)

104° *Gruppo Sparvieri* 253-6 and 253-10 of 253ª *Squadriglia* and a 252ª *Squadriglia* machine form up for the photographer in a fourth S.79 during the summer of 1942

another damaged. In addition to the loss of Annona's machine, the 204ª *Squadriglia* war diary recorded that three S.79s were hit by anti-aircraft fire and three British fighters shot down by return fire.

There was an aftermath to Operation *Harpoon* on 17 June when four 130° *Gruppo* S.79s (Capitano Melley flying 280-6 and three from 283ª *Squadriglia*, flown by Tenenti Cipriani, Focacci and Cossu) attacked the cruiser HMS *Cairo* and the destroyers HMS *Blankney*, HMS *Ithuriel*, HMS *Marne* and HMS *Middleton* 20 miles northwest of Galite at 1110 hrs. The British warships, which had been heading for Gibraltar since 16 June, 'welcomed' the S.79s with a tremendous hail of anti-aircraft fire that prevented any effective torpedo dropping – all of the weapons missed their targets. That evening *Cairo* and its escorts met the cruisers *Charybdis* and HMS *Kenya* and, thus reinforced, the British formation safely entered Gibraltar late the following day.

On 26 June 41° *Gruppo* resumed its offensive sweeps over the eastern Mediterranean when two S.79s flown by Tenenti Luigi Vicariotto of 204ª *Squadriglia* and Giuseppe Briatore of 205ª *Squadriglia* spotted a freighter escorted by a destroyer – the vessels also had two fighters providing top cover. Although Vicariotto did not drop his torpedo because of shallow soundings, Briatore employed his weapon but it failed, probably having sunk in the shallows. His aircraft was then bounced and shot down by British fighters, all of the crew being killed. Briatore's victor was probably Sqn Ldr Paul Evans of No 89 Sqn in Beaufighter X7754, who is credited in some sources with an S.79 kill northeast of Port Said. Not wishing to meet the same fate, Tenente Vicariotto wisely broke off and returned to Rhodes with his torpedo.

July saw 104° *Gruppo* involved in other actions that resulted in it sustaining further losses. On the 14th a 253ª *Squadriglia* S.79 flown by a 252ª *Squadriglia* crew (pilot Tenente Guglielmo Michelotti) ran out of fuel and forced-landed on Gavdos Island. On 25 July another 252ª *Squadriglia* crew aboard a 253ª *Squadriglia* S.79 (pilot Tenente Guido Bresciani) were killed when their aircraft was downed by 805 NAS Martlets, Lt Cdr Goode and Sub Lt Lewis from this unit claiming two *Sparvieri* destroyed.

OPERATION *PEDESTAL*

The partial failure of the June convoys to Malta compelled the Royal Navy to stage another supply operation to the besieged island in August 1942, codenamed *Pedestal*.

During the evening of 11 August nine Beaufighters of No 248 Sqn set off from Malta and successfully attacked Sardinian airfields at Elmas and Decimomannu to prevent the *Regia Aeronautica* from attacking Malta-bound Convoy WS 21S. The low-flying British aircraft struck hard at refuelling Italian torpedo-bombers, destroying five S.79s and damaging another 15. Of the five destroyed *Sparvieri*, one belonged to 283ª *Squadriglia* (130° *Gruppo*), one to 255ª *Squadriglia* (105° *Gruppo*) and three to 36° *Stormo*.

Despite this disastrous attack, the *Aeronautica Sardegna* mustered a remarkable force of 43 torpedo-bombers (33 of them S.79s) and 26 Reggiane Re.2001 escorting fighters. From about 1300 hrs on 12 August this strike force (reduced to 41 aircraft after two 36° *Stormo* S.79s turned back) attacked the *Pedestal* convoy, which had been sighted at 1240 hrs, but unfortunately achieved nothing. Two aircraft were lost, an Re.2001 of 2° *Gruppo Caccia* (flown by Sottotenente Antonio Bizio) being shot down by 801 NAS Sea Hurricane pilot Sub Lt Peter Hutton, and a 36° *Stormo* S.79 torpedo-bomber, flown by 109° *Gruppo* commander Maggiore Alfredo Zanardi, falling to FAA fighters while attacking the battleship HMS *Nelson*. Zanardi's crew took to their raft, but wireless operator Sergente Maggiore Pasquale Rombola had been mortally wounded. They were rescued by a German submarine more than 50 hours later.

This striking photograph shows an S.79 of a *Nucleo Addestramento* (note its all-white engine cowlings) banking over an Italian naval convoy during 1942

Zanardi was leading nine 109° *Gruppo* S.79s as part of a 12-strong formation that included three *Sparvieri* from 2° and 3° *Nuclei AS*, including Tenente Colonnello Cannaviello's aircraft. The 12 *Aerosiluranti* had left Decimomannu at 1125 hrs, and *Sparvieri* of the two *Nuclei Addestramento* shared some torpedo-bomber claims against ships. In fact all of the torpedoes were avoided, the S.79s returning to base at 1335 hrs.

Included in *Aeronautica Sardegna*'s *Sparvieri* attack force were nine 130° *Gruppo* aircraft (four from 280ª and five from 283ª *Squadriglie*), which at 1240 hrs reached the convoy northwest of Galite. The British ships opened fire and several Sea Hurricanes intercepted the formation, Italian gunners claiming one fighter shot down and another as a probable. In this action eight 130° *Gruppo* S.79s (four each from 280ª and 283ª *Squadriglie*) were badly damaged by naval fighters, but the Italians landed back at base at 1635 hrs. As usual, 283ª *Squadriglia*'s formation included 'Ciccio' Di Bella, aboard MM23971/283-6.

Ten minutes after the 109° *Gruppo* aircraft departed Decimomannu, 105° *Gruppo* also sent S.79s into action from the airfield. Its crews subsequently reported seven torpedoes dropped and some *Sparvieri* hit by flak splinters. S.79s 254-3 (flown by Maggiore Francesco Campello) and 254-7 (flown by Sottotenente Ernesto Borrelli) returned to base badly damaged after combat with naval fighters. Among

Two British destroyers of the *Pedestal* escort come under attack by 132° *Gruppo* in the late afternoon of 12 August 1942 (*Aeronautica Militare*)

A 132° *Gruppo* S.79 heads for the *Pedestal* convoy at 1835 hrs on 12 August 1942. In this action *Sparvieri* accounted for the destroyer HMS *Foresight* – their only success of the entire battle. This sinking was credited to a trio of S.79s flown by Capitani Ugo Rivoli and Graziani and Sottotenente Pfister (*Aeronautica Militare*)

the 105° *Gruppo* aircraft that took part in the action were two from 255ª *Squadriglia* (flown by Tenenti Giuseppe Cimicchi and Mario Massera of 3° *Nucleo AS*). All 105° *Gruppo* S.79s returned to Decimomannu between 1400 hrs and 1410 hrs.

Regarding the Sea Hurricane pilots' S.79 claims in this action, 801 NAS's Sub Lt Peter Hutton claimed an S.79 probably destroyed, while squadronmate Lt Cdr Rupert Brabner was credited with a *Sparviero* as a confirmed kill, as was ace Lt Cdr John Bruen of 800 NAS. Fulmar pilot Lt Cdr Frank Pennington of 884 NAS shared in the destruction of an S.79, but his aircraft was damaged by return fire. Martlet pilots Lt Bartlett and Sub Lt Street of 806 NAS claimed one S.79 destroyed apiece. Sub Lt John Lucas of 800 NAS was posted as missing.

That afternoon at 1835 hrs, 14 132° *Gruppo* S.79s (seven each from 278ª and 281ª *Squadriglie*) and nine 102° *Gruppo Tuffatori* Stukas, all escorted by 28 fighters, attacked the convoy again. At 1843 hrs one torpedo struck the 1850-ton destroyer HMS *Foresight*, which, although taken in tow, was scuttled at 0955 hrs the next day by the destroyer HMS *Tartar* due to the damage sustained. Some sources credit *Foresight*'s loss, the only *Aerosiluranti* 'kill' during Operation *Pedestal*, to a 132° *Gruppo* patrol made up of Capitani Ugo Rivoli and Giulio Cesare Graziani and Sottotenente Carlo Pfister.

Seven 132° *Gruppo* S.79s were damaged by the fierce naval barrage put up by the convoy, but worse came shortly after the unit had landed at Pantelleria. At dusk three No 248 Sqn Beaufighters, flown by Sub Lt G P R Weil, Plt Off P St C Bate and Sgt R W Sebring, surprised the 132° *Gruppo Sparvieri* on the ground and strafed them. One S.79 was set ablaze and two others, one S.84 and a Ju 52/3m were all damaged – 28 fuel drums were also blown up. Sottotenente Vittorio Moretti was struck by a burst of machine gun fire, which threw him against a revolving propeller of his S.79, killing him instantly. A bomb splinter also wounded photographer Aviere Scelto Giuseppe Caringella (from Tenente Paolo Manfredi's crew) in the head.

Despite this attack, 132° *Gruppo* attacked the convoy again the following day (13 August) with five aircraft, led by Capitano Ugo Rivoli. One torpedo became entangled in the paravane of the steamer *Port Chalmers,* which was then narrowly missed by another weapon. There was no luck for the torpedo-bombers, however, as they were attacked by four Malta-based No 126 Sqn Spitfire Vs during their escape. In the ensuing fight the S.79 flown by Tenente Guido Barani was shot down in flames, the pilot and his crew being killed. Its loss, however, should be shared between fighters and naval fire, for although ace Wg Cdr Prosser Hanks

55

claimed to have scored strikes on the S.79, which was then finished off by fellow ace Plt Off Rod Smith, gunners aboard the destroyers HMS *Pathfinder* and *Tartar* almost certainly shared in the aircraft's destruction as the ships claimed a torpedo-bomber shot down apiece.

That same day at 1325 hrs, Tenente Colonnello Cannaviello (in S.79 280-5) led five *Sparvieri* – three from 130° and two from 105° *Gruppi* – against British ships near Bougie. Although S.79 254-4, flown by Tenente Michele Avalle, was forced to turn back when his wing engines started to play up, the four remaining *Sparvieri* targeted the cruiser HMS *Nigeria* and its four escort destroyers at 1520 hrs. Despite the cruiser having already been badly damaged by the Italian submarine *Axum*, a violent naval barrage hit the attackers. The flak forced Sottotenente Manlio Caresio's 280-12 to turn sharply at the instant it dropped its torpedo, which went astray. The other three S.79s launched their torpedoes from a range of 800 m (875 yds), although *Nigeria* avoided them all. Capitano Urbano Mancini (in 254-2) of 254ª *Squadriglia* and Sottotenente Caresio of 280ª *Squadriglia* both claimed torpedo hits, however. Although the fourth aircraft, flown by Tenente 'Ciccio' Di Bella, was damaged by flak its crew dropped their torpedo, to no avail.

Aerosiluranti losses during Operation *Pedestal* reached their peak on 13 August when two 255ª *Squadriglia* (105° *Gruppo*) S.79s – flown by Capitano Giulio Ricciarini and Tenente Silvio Angelucci – were shot down by anti-aircraft fire from the British destroyer HMS *Ledbury*. Angelucci and his crew were lost, but Ricciarini's crew survived after their pilot managed to ditch their *Sparviero* despite it being struck several times and set on fire. They were saved 21 hrs later by a Cant Z.506B rescue seaplane of 612ª *Squadriglia* flown by Maresciallo Dario Tomassi. Before they had been shot down both S.79 crews had managed to drop their torpedoes. Tenente Angelucci was posthumously awarded the Gold Medal for Military Valour following his death. The double S.79 kill for *Ledbury* was credited to Leading Seaman Douglas Meakin and Able Seaman Arthur James, pom-pom and Oerlikon gunners, respectively.

Capitano Ricciarini recalled this episode some time later;

'At 1400 hrs I was ordered to carry out a torpedo reconnaissance. Tenente Silvio Angelucci was my companion in the action, as right wingman. I headed for Africa, and after 45 minutes I sighted smoke on the horizon. Approaching the target (there were crippled ships in the area) I saw three big oil slicks caused by the sinking of three steamers. I went on, and after ten minutes, near Cape Bon, I sighted an enemy cruiser heading west at eight knots.

'I started my attack, and at about 800 m [875 yds] range I dropped the torpedo just as a burst of 20 mm cannon fire struck my aircraft. I initially thought that it had hit the right engine, but I soon saw that the right wing fuel tank was on fire. I ordered my co-pilot Tenente Nicola Titi to pull out the fire extinguisher as a precautionary measure, but the blaze soon grew in intensity and I decided to ditch at once. I was trusting in the support of the second aircraft while I looked for somewhere to ditch, Tenente Angelucci having positioned his S.79 about a kilometre away from me. As I turned away from the vessels and glided towards the water, I saw Tenente Angelucci's aircraft fly over the cruiser at low level, increasingly losing altitude.

'My aircraft was literally wrapped in flames and smoke. I saw my co-pilot, outlined in the cockpit's choking greyness, abandon his seat after

On 13 August 1942 Tenente Silvio Angelucci of 105° *Gruppo*'s 255ª *Squadriglia* was killed in action along with his crew by anti-aircraft fire from the destroyer HMS *Ledbury*. This episode saw the Royal Navy vessel score a double kill, as its accurate flak also downed the 255ª *Squadriglia* S.79 flown by Capitano Giulio Ricciarini, whose crew survived. As Angelucci had managed to drop his torpedo before his S.79 was downed, he was posthumously awarded the *Medaglia d'Oro al Valor Militare* (*Aeronautica Militare*)

he had sustained severe burns to his left hand. Given that I had almost no visibility out of the cockpit, I ditched almost by instinct. As we hit the water I was thrown into the torpedo-aiming sight, injuring my nose. At once the water flowed into the cockpit and, luckily, extinguished the fuel tank fire. Unable to open the cockpit roof, I then had to remove my parachute so that I could crawl inside the fuselage. Here, I saw a crewman lying on his back. I lifted him up and, believing he was dead, decided to leave him there. The raft was still on board.

'Although I couldn't swim, I reached the fuselage hatch and threw myself into the water. Then I saw the rest of the crew, who had gathered on the port wing. I held onto the aircraft with one hand and used the other to try and remove the raft from its housing and put it into the sea. After several attempts, and with the crew's help, I managed to pull the dinghy out. The aircraft's fuselage fabric had been burnt away and just its skeleton was left, through which I saw a crewman who I hadn't previously spotted in the smoke. It was flight engineer Aviere Scelto Tedeschini, who showed signs of life despite his legs clearly being on fire. I threw water on him and managed to extinguish the flames.

'Wireless operator Aviere Scelto Bruno Bianconi managed to inflate the dinghy using an oxygen cylinder, while Tenente Titi rescued Tedeschini and recovered ration boxes, throwing them towards us into the water. 1° Aviere Corrado Celeste recovered the camera and threw it to me, but it ended up in the water Although the dinghy had been holed by a machine gun round, we put the unconscious flight engineer in it first and then climbed aboard just as the aircraft started to sink – 15 minutes had passed since the ditching. We were now alone on the vast expanse of water.

'I was told by my crew that Tenente Angelucci's aircraft had been set on fire before our S.79.'

One of the final *Pedestal* attacks that day was mounted by two S.79s of 3° *Nucleo AS* that had taken off from Chinisia at about 1430 hrs. The lead aircraft was flown by Capitano Dante Magagnoli, who attacked the British freighter *Brisbane Star* in Hammamet Gulf. The torpedoes launched by both *Sparvieri* disappeared without trace, however.

That same day 104° *Gruppo* attacked diversionary Convoy MG 3 in the eastern Mediterranean. Three 253ª *Squadriglia* S.79s (flown by Capitano Solimena, Tenente Marescalchi and Sottotenente Del Ponte) targeted the cruisers HMS *Cleopatra* and HMS *Arethusa* and the destroyers HMS *Sikh*, HMS *Zulu*, HMS *Javelin* and HMS *Kelvin*. The trio of *Sparvieri* were forced to give up their attack when confronted by top-cover Beaufighters and a fierce ack-ack barrage from the naval vessels.

On 14 August eight S.79s flew the last action in the *Pedestal* battle, but achieved no results. Although the Allies had suffered heavy losses and the Axis forces had earned a tactical success, the Royal Navy achieved the strategic one (this is contested by some sources), providing Malta with vital supplies. One of the Italian airmen decorated for his deeds during *Pedestal* was Tenente Francesco Di Bella, who received his fifth Silver Medal. On 7 October Di Bella left 130° *Gruppo* for 3° *Nucleo AS*, where he served as a flying instructor alongside his friend Tenente Roberto Cipriani.

During Operation *Pedestal* 93 Italian torpedo-bombers from Sardinia and Sicily had flown 110 sorties against the convoy, dropping 87 torpedoes but scoring only one success.

On 18 August, several days after *Pedestal* had ended, two 253[a] *Squadriglia* S.79s flown by Tenenti Enrico Marescalchi and Vittorio Marotta attacked the destroyer HMS *Paladin* as it was proceeding at high speed south of Cyprus. Marescalchi dropped his torpedo at 800 m (875 yds) range, but *Paladin* avoided it with a skilful manoeuvre. The destroyer's ack-ack took its toll on the attackers, damaging Marescalchi's S.79 and shooting down Marotta's aircraft, its crew being picked up and captured. Tenente Marotta later recalled;

'I was flying at low altitude as Tenente Marescalchi's wingman when I spotted to my right either a destroyer or a cruiser – I later discovered that it was the destroyer *Paladin*. I reported its presence to Tenente Marescalchi, who prepared himself for the attack approach manoeuvre, trying to aim at the ship's bow. I at once separated from him and started the required attack manoeuvre, increasing speed, while the destroyer opened fire at both aircraft. From then on I lost sight of Tenente Marescalchi as I set about making the same attack. Because of the ship's evasive manoeuvres I repeated my approach three times, managing only on the third attempt to get into an excellent release position.

'Once we were at close range, and while the gunner tried to disturb the ship's defensive fire, I ordered my "second" [co-pilot] to drop the torpedo. Unfortunately the drop didn't work, and I just had time to make another attempt – still unsuccessful – when the wings, fuselage and both engines were struck, the motors immediately becoming useless. With the torpedo still in its rack and the aircraft by now nearly over the target, there was nothing to do but to try and ditch. With a lot of luck I managed this successfully. Although wounded, we all survived the ditching – I had a splinter in my forehead and my gunner was knocked around when we hit the sea, suffering slight injuries and several bruises.

'We had the time to float the raft and climb aboard, although the flight engineer failed to do so. I searched for him in the now flooded fuselage while the aircraft's buoyancy rapidly decreased. Luckily, the crew called to me that the flight engineer was swimming towards the raft – in the impact he had been thrown into the water. I just had time to jump onto the raft when the aircraft suddenly sank. After about an hour we were picked up by the *Paladin* and, together with my deputy, I was separated from the rest of my crew, whom I did not see again.

'My wound was initially treated aboard the ship, and I was disembarked the following day at Port Said, whence I was sent to Geneifa PoW camp on the Suez Canal and admitted to the annexed hospital. Here, I was treated by Italian medical officers, who served there as "protected personnel".'

Afterwards, Tenente Marotta was sent to a PoW camp in India. He was eventually repatriated on 18 August 1946 following four years of imprisonment.

OPERATION *TORCH*

After almost three months of inactivity, the S.79 torpedo-bomber units were hastily prepared to repel the anticipated Allied landing in North Africa (codenamed Operation *Torch*). On 6 November, just 48 hours before the Allies came ashore in Vichy French Morocco and Algeria, 132° *Gruppo* moved to Sicily with 18 S.79s. Sardinian-based 105° and 130° *Gruppi* had 37 airworthy S.79s between them on this date, and they were joined that

Violent anti-aircraft fire 'welcomes' the *Aerosiluranti* over Bougie Bay. On 11 November 1942 such a barrage shot down Sottotenente Ramiro Angelucci's S.79 of 132° *Gruppo*, killing the crew. According to Maggiore Gabriele Casini, this photograph was taken from Capitano Graziani's *Sparviero* (*Aeronautica Militare*)

same day by 15 S.79s from 36° *Stormo Aerosiluranti*, 25 S.84s from 32° *Stormo Aerosiluranti* and five S.79s from 3° *Nucleo Addestramento*.

The 'hunchbacks' began operations against Allied shipping on the afternoon of 8 November, when 14 S.79s were despatched from Sardinia. However, the *Sparvieri* enjoyed no success, with one 105° *Gruppo* aircraft (254-6 of Tenente Antonio Poggi Cavalletti) being lost over Algiers. This dramatic mission also involved Capitano Mancini in 254-2 and Tenente Michele Avalle in 254-7.

Later that same day three 280ª and six 283ª *Squadriglie Sparvieri*, led by Capitano Franco Melley in 280-13, attacked targets at 1830 hrs, but all of the 130° *Gruppo* S.79s were hit by anti-aircraft fire. During their return flight 280-3 (flown by Tenente Alessandro Setti) and 283-10 (Sottotenente Antonio Vellere), which had had their tanks holed by flak, were forced to ditch. Setti descended in the Cagliari Gulf, and his crew reached the shore in their dinghy after some hours at sea. Vellere's S.79 ditched in the Elmas Pond inlet, the slightly wounded crew later being rescued by a *Regia Aeronautica* motor launch.

On 9 and 11 November Tenente 'Ciccio' Di Bella of 3° *Nucleo AS* dropped his torpedoes against ships off the Algerian coast, but to no avail. The *Sparvieris'* first real success came between these dates during the afternoon of 10 November when five 130° *Gruppo* S.79s (three from 280ª and two from 283ª *Squadriglie*) led by Maggiore Massimiliano Erasi (in 280-6) sank the 1250-ton British sloop HMS *Ibis* ten miles north of Algiers – 98 of its 200 crew were lost. One of the attackers was Tenente Cimicchi in 283-4.

On the 11th a German reconnaissance aircraft spotted numerous Allied ships in Bougie Bay. The first aircraft to attack them were four S.79s of 132° *Gruppo Aerosiluranti*, flown by Maggiore Buscaglia, Capitano Giulio Cesare Graziani, Tenente Carlo Faggioni and Sottotenente Ramiro Angelucci. The four *Aerosiluranti* failed to achieve any results, with Angelucci's *Sparviero* being shot down by Allied anti-aircraft fire and all of its crew killed. That afternoon three 254ª and two 255ª *Squadriglie Sparvieri* of 105° *Gruppo* were in action off the Bougie area. Anti-aircraft fire hit Tenente Olindo Casanova's 254-9, which was flying with Capitano Mancini's 254-2 and Tenente Avalle's 254-1. Following the attack, Tenente Alessandro Senni and Sottotenente Giuseppe Leonardi of 255ª *Squadriglia* both crash-landed.

On 12 November Buscaglia attacked Bougie again, leading six torpedo-bombers of 132° *Gruppo* off from Castelvetrano airfield at 1050 hrs. To avoid interception the S.79s, flown by Maggiore Buscaglia, Tenente Francesco Bargagna and Sottotenenti Carlo Pfister, Martino Aichner, Marino Marini and Giuseppe Coci, took a longer southerly route, then headed north after penetrating deeply inland in order to take the enemy by surprise from the rear.

Even so, the Italians were intercepted by No 81 Sqn Spitfires scrambled from Djidjelli airfield. The fighters flown by Flg Off Large and Plt Off Rigby riddled Buscaglia's aircraft with bullets, instantly killing gunner 1° Aviere Armiere Walter Vecchiarelli and wireless operator Maresciallo Edmondo Balestri. Although his trimotor was in flames, Buscaglia stubbornly aimed at a steamer, dropped a torpedo and then crashed straight into the water. Co-pilot Sergente Maggiore Francesco Sogliuzzo and flight engineer 1° Aviere Motorista Vittorio Vercesi died in the crash. The remaining 132° *Gruppo* S.79s disengaged from the fray as best they could, returning fire at the pursuing Spitfires. Three of the RAF aircraft were hit, Plt Off Byford crash-landing at Djidjelli with wounds, while Flg Off Large and Plt Off Rigby crashed on either side of Bougie Bay. The British recorded the three Spitfires as being lost to their own anti-aircraft fire, however.

Buscaglia later recalled his dramatic shootdown;

'At 1430 hrs we arrived over the target [according to another source, Buscaglia's patrol reached Bougie Bay at 1355 hrs]. I launched the torpedo at an enemy vessel and strafed the decks of other ships. I couldn't observe the result exactly. At that moment I found myself isolated. The other five aircraft, I don't know why, had spread out. I saw them four or five kilometres away.

'A formation of Spitfires – I counted more than seven – jumped on to me and I had to engage them in combat. The tail gunner and the wireless operator were killed instantly. The rear machine guns no longer worked, the aircraft having been set alight. Wrapped in flames, it crashed into the water from a height of 70 to 80 metres [230-260 ft]. I was unconscious, and I don't know how I kept floating. Photographer Maiore was close to me but the others burned on the water. Two hours later Maiore and I were picked up by a British unit engaged in the action. We remained untended all afternoon, through the night and the next morning. Then we were transported to a French hospital in the Bougie area. My companion's condition was very bad, and I had bad burns to my feet, legs, hands and face. I was deprived of sight for 30 days. On 15 November we were moved to an English military hospital near Bougie. On 27 November Maiore passed away after atrocious suffering.

'After the first few days the English took a little better care of me. On 28 November I was transferred to another hospital, where I received excellent care and was operated on by a renowned surgeon. In that hospital I was interrogated by an American officer of the Allied Headquarters, who asked me about the Italian Air Force's situation, Italy's war aims and my own political and military opinions. I replied that, as a prisoner of war, I couldn't release any information to the enemy.'

The fact that Buscaglia remained isolated from the remaining S.79s during the Bougie Bay attack was also reported by his two wingmen, Sottotenenti Aichner and Giuseppe Coci, who explained that they were unable to follow their leader closely because he was flying at full throttle. Aichner later recalled the action;

'In my earphones I could hear my commander's quiet voice. "In a single line, spaced to avoid slipstream". A short while later he radioed, "Come into attack formation". Suddenly before us appeared the endless and bright sea, with a roof of identical white clouds. We were overlooking the bay from a balcony more than 1000 metres high, peering through a hole among the clouds and the mountains that was no more than 100 metres high and wide.

Although he had been wounded in action the day before, photographer Aviere Scelto Francesco Maiore insisted that he accompany Maggiore Buscaglia on his ill-fated mission over Bougie on 12 November 1942. An Allied craft rescued him, badly burned, after his S.79 had been downed, and Maiore suffered agonising pain prior to dying in an Allied hospital 15 days later. Maiore's faithful devotion to duty, and to his commander, earned him a posthumous *Medaglia d'Oro al Valor Militare* (*Aeronautica Militare*)

A rear view of an aerial torpedo slung under an S.79, clearly showing the weapon's wooden aerodynamic tail stabilisers that were shed once the weapon had splashed into the water (*SME*)

'We dropped down behind the commander, but even at full speed we couldn't reach him. The first Spitfires singled out the leader and struck him with their opening bursts. Fire immediately broke out in his aircraft. I was behind Buscaglia when his S.79 was hit. I was a little out of line because although I was at full throttle, I had been unable to catch him. During the enemy fighters' first pass I instinctively tried to increase speed, pressing the handwheel to get close to him. I gained a few tenths of metres but I lost altitude. I could see the underside of the S.79, and the carousel of Spitfires attacking him, ignoring us wingmen. They had realised that Buscaglia's aeroplane was the bigger prey.'

Aichner's account is at odds with the description of events given by 1° Aviere Armiere Rosario Salvatore D'Angelo, the gunner aboard Sottotenente Pfister's aircraft;

'Maggiore Buscaglia waggled his aircraft's wings – this was the signal that the formation could open out, each crew choosing its target and dropping its torpedo, possibly to strike. The other four wingmen obeyed the order and, dropping further, we saw them heading away for the targets. Nothing more of them was seen until our return to base. However, our pilot, Sottotenente Pfister, still lingered, keeping himself close to the leader's wing. He had correctly guessed Buscaglia's thoughts – "Inside that hell, in Bougie's port, there's my target!"

'Pfister gazed around into the fuselage as if questioning his flying companions. At that instant of perfect harmony he understood that one thought was in all our minds – together, close to the commander, where duty calls. Suddenly, the flak bursts and the crackle of splinters on our aircraft's fuselage and wings ceased. The two torpedo-bombers, as if tied wing-to-wing, moved towards their selected prey in that false silence. Speed was at its highest, having applied the "+200" [maximum speed device]. In the aircraft we could smell fuel – the consequence of activation of the maximum speed device, caused by the escape of gas from the little vent pipe [of the fuel tanks] located near the dorsal turret.

'Once the flak stopped, numerous enemy P-40s and Hurricanes [actually Spitfires] went after the two torpedo-bombers, and the crackling on our aircraft's fuselage resumed. The attacks came from all directions, but mainly from the left. At some point an enemy fighter broke off, trailing black smoke and heading for the ground, its pilot looking for an emergency landing site. The balance was still in our favour, but the enemies were always overwhelming.

'The sun, when the flak ceased, pierced the dirty haze and returned to shine. However, now it was our ally because it beat inexorably on the windscreens of the fighters coming from the left. Suddenly a P-40 stumbled into the crossfire of our machine guns. A trail of smoke and flames accompanied the fighter until it impacted the sea. Then my turret gun failed. A swift glance down showed that the belt feed had run out of ammunition. I rushed aft to man the port waist machine gun instead, and it was now necessary to fire measured bursts as my shots were precious to the aircraft's defence. A distressing thought gripped me. What if I was to run out of ammunition here too?

'Finally we arrived at a range of about 700 m [770 yds] from our target and dropped the torpedo. At that same instant Maggiore Buscaglia turned left, but an explosion in the fuselage wrapped his aircraft in smoke and flames. The S.79 slipped over onto one wing and "caressed" the water, which (as we learnt subsequently) extinguished the fire and saved our commander's life.'

Afterwards, while his crewmen checked the damage to their aircraft, Pfister's S.79 made it back to Castelvetrano. According to 1° Aviere Armiere D'Angelo, Pfister was the last to land there, at 1630 hrs. The 132° *Gruppo* war diary reported that the mission ended at 1610 hrs.

In respect to disagreements in the various reports, one probable explanation could be that Buscaglia was concentrating so hard on his target that he did not notice Pfister. However, even taking into account the inevitable confusion during an aerial battle, it is strange that Pfister was not seen by Aichner and Coci. In fact the latter, having asked Aichner for his mission account, stated;

'Meanwhile, the formation wasn't compact but loose, as Maggiore Buscaglia, coming out over the gulf, had given full throttle and thrown himself down headlong. We of the second patrol [Bargagna, Pfister and Coci] were soon detached by more than 1000 metres, Buscaglia ahead of you [Aichner] and Marini. I saw at a distance the Commander's aircraft, which was leaving a trail of black smoke. Then the flight engineer said to me, "The Commander has plunged into the sea in flames". When I was 600/700 metres from a steamer, which was outside the port, I dropped the torpedo. I noticed the water was boiling beneath me and, knowing the fighters had attacked me, I threw my aircraft towards the open sea and set a solitary course for home.'

Of the last moments of Buscaglia's aircraft, Aichner added;

'Marini and I followed Buscaglia in line. He was flying a straight trajectory, which was quite different from his usual method of making abrupt manoeuvres to avoid enemy gunfire. It was clear to us that the

Maggiore Carlo Emanuele Buscaglia, seen here with the rank of capitano, displays his numerous decorations – six Silver Medals for Military Valour and two war merit promotions, including the Iron Cross 2nd Class ribbon. Shot down on 12 November 1942 over Bougie Bay by No 81 Sqn Spitfires, he survived, although seriously injured. Captured and imprisoned in the USA, he resumed fighting on the Allied side. After repatriation Buscaglia assumed command of 28° *Gruppo* within the ICAF *Stormo Baltimore*. Tragically, on 23 August 1944 his Baltimore bomber crashed on takeoff from Naples' Campo Vesuvio airfield and he died of his injuries the following day. The *Medaglia d'Oro al Valor Militare*, awarded for the Bougie action, recognised his outstanding service and courage (*via author*)

aircraft was no longer controlled, but was heading towards the harbour for a desperate ditching.'

Initially, Buscaglia was listed as killed, but, as related earlier in this chapter, he was picked up along with photographer Aviere Scelto Francesco Maiore, both having been badly burned. The unfortunate and faithful Maiore, despite having been wounded the day before, had chosen to follow his commander into battle once again. This act of devotion earned him a posthumous award of the Gold Medal for Military Valour.

Buscaglia was sent to a US PoW camp in Crossville, Tennessee, and he later agreed to join the pro-Allied ICAF, being repatriated in April 1944. Once in Italy he took command of 28° *Gruppo* of *Aeronautica Cobelligerante*. However, on 23 August 1944 he crashed a Martin Baltimore twin-engined bomber while trying to take off from Campo Vesuvio (Naples) airfield. Buscaglia extricated himself from the blazing aircraft, but was badly injured and died in hospital the next day. The well-deserved awarding of the *Medaglia d'Oro al Valor Militare* for his last Bougie action was rightful recognition of his outstanding courage.

On the day of Buscaglia's loss on 12 November 1942, four 280ª and five 283ª *Squadriglie Sparvieri*, led by Capitano Franco Melley (in 280-6), attacked a convoy in Bougie Bay at 1800 hrs. Naval gunfire brought down Sottotenente Nino Meschiari (in 280-2), but not before he had dropped the torpedo from his blazing S.79. Four days later, at 1040 hrs, three 105° *Gruppo* S.79s (one from 254ª and two from 255ª *Squadriglie*) led by Tenente Nicola Titi made an attacking sweep between Cape de Fer and Bougie. The 255ª *Squadriglia* S.79s flown by Tenenti Titi and Lorenzo Gangemi failed to return, having fallen to Spitfire VBs of Nos 154 and 242 Sqns. The units actually claimed three S.79s between them, shared by Flt Lt Geoffrey Harrison and ace Flg Off Alan Aikman of No 154 Sqn and ace Flt Lt Douglas Benham and Plt Offs Hampshire and Mather of No 242 Sqn.

Capitano Giulio Cesare Graziani took temporary command of 132° *Gruppo Aerosiluranti* on 20 November, the unit being designated *Gruppo* 'Buscaglia' in honour of its famous commander – it fought under this name until the armistice of 8 September 1943. That same day seven 132° *Gruppo* S.79s led by Capitano Graziani flew the unit's first night torpedo action. At 1745 hrs the *Sparvieri* attacked shipping in Philippeville Bay, achieving nothing despite three hits claimed. During their return flight they were attacked by five Beaufighters from No 46 Sqn, and another S.79 (flown by Sottotenente Giuseppe Coci), which had been hit by ack-ack, was forced to ditch off Tunisia, its crew reaching shore safely.

At 0300 hrs (Italian time) on 23 November three 130° *Gruppo* S.79s attacked vessels in Algiers Bay. Despite dangerous anti-aircraft fire, Sottotenenti Francesco Cossu in 283-9 and Antonio Vellere in 283-7 claimed two freighters hit (one sunk and one damaged). The British reported that the large 19,761-ton steamer *Scythia* had indeed been damaged off Algiers by a torpedo at 0400 hrs (British time, corresponding to the time of the Italian attack). Other sources suggest that possible claimants for this attack could be I./KG 26's He 111 torpedo-bombers, which targeted the *Scythia* at 1930 hrs and 0330 hrs.

Shortly before noon on 24 November, six S.79s (three each from 105° and 108° *Gruppi*) left Decimomannu to attack shipping near Cape Bougaroun, but no hits were scored. One aircraft from 257ª *Squadriglia*

(108° *Gruppo*), flown by Sottotenente Romano Bazza, failed to return, probably falling to anti-aircraft fire. All of its crew were lost. Later that same day three 280ª *Squadriglia Sparvieri* that had taken off at 1230 hrs claimed two 6000-ton steamers sunk and another hit southwest of Cape Bougaroun. Despite fierce anti-aircraft fire, all three (280-9, 280-10 and 280-13, flown by Tenenti Setti, Lo Prieno and Tredici, respectively) landed back at base at 1620 hrs.

On 25 November four 132° *Gruppo* S.79s left Castelvetrano for Sardinian Villacidro, while three 1° *Nucleo AS Sparvieri* departed Decimomannu and returned to their home base at Gorizia. That same day nine S.79s from 105° and 108° *Gruppi* and 280ª *Squadriglia* (130° *Gruppo*) flew anti-shipping sweeps off the Algerian coast but achieved nothing.

Three days later, on 28 November, Sardinia's *Aerosiluranti* attacked a convoy spotted off the Algerian coast between Algiers and Bougie. The first action saw Tenente Francesco Di Bella of 3° *Nucleo AS* airborne with Capitano Giulio Marini and Tenente Vezio Terzi. This trio (all flying S.79s from 108° *Gruppo*) was joined by three S.79s from 132° *Gruppo* (flown by Capitano Giulio Cesare Graziani and Sottotenenti Carlo Pfister and Martino Aichner). The six 132° *Gruppo Sparvieri* shared in the sinking of the 1774-ton Norwegian steamer *Selbo*. Anti-aircraft fire damaged the undercarriage of Pfister's S.79 and slightly wounded a crewman. Shortly after this mission Graziani was posted as an instructor to 1° *Nucleo AS* at Gorizia.

In the second action against the convoy, at 1445 hrs, three 283ª *Squadriglia* S.79s led by Tenente Cimicchi in 283-9 were intercepted by a single Spitfire of No 154 Sqn. The Spitfire's pilot, New Zealander Flg Off H W 'Paddy' Chambers, claimed four S.79s destroyed, making him an ace and earning him a DFC. He actually only shot down S.79 283-3, flown by Sottotenente Michele Virdis, killing all of the crew. Tenente Cimicchi described this dramatic episode;

'The sky over the area was controlled by enemy fighters. In order not to be seen, we went in at wavetop height and thus managed, incredibly, to exploit the element of surprise. Torpedoes were dropped and some struck home. In fact the explosions alerted the Spitfires, which jumped us, immersing us in a hail of bullets. Sottotenente Virdis' aircraft, which had straggled during the escape, was stricken and set alight, crashing into the sea. Hit by an enemy bullet, the central engine of my aircraft stopped working, but I managed to return to base.'

DECEMBER SLAUGHTER

Six 130° *Gruppo* S.79s led by Capitano Melley were airborne at 0855 hrs on 2 December to intercept a British naval formation sighted north of Bizerte. Nearly an hour after takeoff the starboard engine of Melley's 280-6 failed, forcing him to abort the mission. Tragically, the five remaining *Sparvieri* were intercepted by two No 242 Sqn Spitfires flown by Plt Offs Hamblin and Lindsay. The British pilots claimed three Savoias downed and a fourth damaged (four were actually lost). Apparently ace Wg Cdr Petrus Hugo, CO of No 322 Wing, also participated in this combat, as he claimed two kills as well.

Sparvieri 280-11 of Tenente Lo Prieno, 280-10 of Sottotenente Vellere, 283-2 of Sottotenente Ingrosso (all crewmen killed) and 280-13 of

On 2 December 1942 Sottotenente Antonio Vellere, under a hail of fire from Spitfires from No 242 Sqn, kept his aircraft, 280-10, in formation for as long as he could before finally crashing into the Mediterranean. For his bravery Vellere received a posthumous *Medaglia d'Oro al Valor Militare* (*Aeronautica Militare*)

A trio of 280ª *Squadriglia* S.79s are seen in flight off Sardinia in 1942, *Sparviero* 280-11 being closest to the camera. According to the *squadriglia* war diary, MM24093 280-11, flown by Tenente Ferruccio Lo Prieno, was one of the four S.79s shot down on 2 December 1942 by No 242 Sqn Spitfires, all of its crew being killed. Lo Prieno devised the 130° *Gruppo* badge, featuring a plump pirate riding a torpedo (*via author*)

Tenente Caresio fell into the sea in succession. These kills were paid for with the loss of Plt Off Hamblin's Spitfire (pilot missing). According to Cimicchi's evidence Hamblin fell to the fire of Aviere Aldo Manca, Tenente Caresio's wireless operator, who also died in this action (he was posthumously awarded the Silver Medal for Military Valour). However, the 130° *Gruppo* and 280ª *Squadriglia* war diaries credit Hamblin's loss to Cimicchi's damaged *Sparviero*.

Sottotenente Antonio Vellere, under the Spitfires' hail of fire, kept his aircraft in formation to the end. For his bravery Vellere received a posthumous Gold Medal for Military Valour. Another pilot lost was Tenente Ferruccio Lo Prieno, creator of the 130° *Gruppo* unit badge (a pirate riding a torpedo). The tragic action was recalled by Tenente Giuseppe Cimicchi (flying 280-5), although he greatly exaggerates the number of Spitfires involved;

'Here they are, the fighters – they are 13 Spitfire IXs [they were in fact combat-weary Spitfire Vs], the latest type, really new and bright. They jump upon us from all sides, firing on us without giving us a break, one, two, three times. The first to be hit is Tenente Lo Prieno's aircraft. "Lo Prieno is falling!" my co-pilot cries. I see the aircraft catch fire, explode, fall off on a wing and sink. The Spitfires resume their assaults. How long will this hell last, and how many of us will follow Lo Prieno? The enemy fighters are evidently trying to scatter our formation, isolating and encircling single torpedo-bombers.

'We are able to advance as a compact formation. But the terrible enemy fire continues – 13 Spitfires, with all their weapons, against us, against our four surviving aircraft. "Vellere's aircraft is burning!" my co-pilot cries again. It's true, but it isn't enough, for I see flames spewing from Tenente Ingrosso's aircraft too. The two aircraft seem to struggle with the fire for some moments, pulling up, fighting their destiny, but in vain. One at a time they too are exploding, falling and plunging into the sea, where they continue to burn.

'Thirteen Spitfires now are vomiting all their firepower at my aircraft and at Caresio's, and we close in on each other as if seeking protection, and go low, zigzagging over the surface of the water to avoid the enemy's attacks. But the 13 Spitfires, like a pack of dogs excited by the smell of blood, are more aggressive than ever. Are they invulnerable? No, at last one of them, struck by our gunfire, catches fire and plunges into the sea.

'Flying as we are a few metres above the sea's surface, we see the water seething with spray under the hailstorm of enemy fire. One Spitfire has threaded its way between Caresio's aircraft and mine. Caresio is challenged to a duel. At the machine gun is wireless operator airman Aldo Manca, a good, brave boy. He has a good aim, for the British fighter is hit and breaks away, its tail smoking. But Manca too is fatally hit. He will be awarded a posthumous Silver Medal.

'The Spitfire pilots seem satisfied with the outcome, or maybe they're afraid of suffering more losses. Anyway, they go. I celebrate with Caresio, shaking my raised and coupled fists towards him in the manner of a boxer. Caresio responds in the same way. Miraculously, we're alive, but we certainly cannot continue with our operation.

'We head for our base with dismay in our hearts. But the adventure isn't over yet. The right wing of Caresio's aircraft, hit during the battle, now burns up. "He doesn't realise it. We must warn him!", I cry. I begin to gesticulate. Caresio sees me and realises what's happening. His calmness is fantastic. He reduces speed, releases the torpedo and prepares to glide onto the waves. Before beginning the manoeuvre he nods to me as if to say "Send someone to pick me up". He glides, then ditches with an appalling crash, but the aircraft stays afloat. The crew has time to move into the raft – one dead and two wounded are among them.

'They'll remain at sea for at least 78 hours, tormented by thirst and starvation. The rescue, initiated by me as soon as we returned to base, could not be achieved any earlier. A German seaplane, escorted by two Messerschmitts, rescued them when they were almost on the verge of insanity. After escaping such an adventurous sinking, poor Caresio died two years later in a trivial flying accident. When I returned to base from that disastrous action on 2 December my aircraft was the only survivor of five torpedo-bombers.'

This slaughter was partly redeemed on 9 December by three S.79s of 105° Gruppo's 254ª *Squadriglia* led by Capitano Urbano Mancini in 254-1, with Tenente Ernesto Borrelli in 254-7 and Sottotenente Olindo Casanova in 254-4 as wingmen. After taking off at 1305 hrs, the three *Sparvieri* attacked a convoy in Algiers Bay, sinking the 925-ton British corvette HMS *Marigold*. The S.79s were then set upon by fighters in a 40-minute combat, the Italians claiming one 'P-40' destroyed. This action might relate to an S.79 kill credited to No 81 Sqn Spitfire VC ace Sqn Ldr Ronald Berry, although his claim was reported on 10 December.

9 December also saw 132° *Gruppo* leave Decimomannu for Sicilian Trapani-Chinisia, thus ending the unit's anti-shipping tour in North African waters.

Three days later one 280ª and two 283ª *Squadriglie Sparvieri* searching for an enemy naval formation were attacked by fighters identified by the Italians as P-40s. In the ensuing combat one of the Allied machines was claimed as downed by return fire from Sottotenente Salvatore Giarrizzo's S.79 280-8. Following this action *Sparvieri* were back at Elmas by 1300 hrs.

For 130° *Gruppo* 1942 ended with two anti-shipping sorties between Cape Bougaroun and Algiers on 21 and 27 December, which proved unsuccessful despite sinking claims.

1943 – YEAR OF DESTINY

1943 was to prove to be the critical year in Italy's war, and it started with a perfectly ordinary service event for the *Aerosiluranti*. At the beginning of January Francesco Di Bella, now promoted to capitano, arrived at Kalamaki airfield in Greece to give nightflying training to 104° *Gruppo*'s Gadurra-based pilots. This had been successfully accomplished by the beginning of March 1943.

An early action for the S.79 torpedo-bombers came on the night of 22 January when six *Sparvieri* of 105° and 132° *Gruppi* attacked ships in Bone harbour. One aircraft, flown by 132° *Gruppo* CO Maggiore Gabriele Casini, had its fuel tanks badly damaged by enemy fighters. The stricken aircraft disengaged, flying at wavetop height, but after an hour it was hit again by naval ack-ack. All three engines now stopped, forcing the pilot to ditch 15 miles off Cape Spartivento. The crew, all wounded, took to the dinghy and were rescued at 0630 hrs the next morning by an Italian merchantman.

On 27 January five 105° and 130° *Gruppi* S.79s flew an armed reconnaissance off Algiers, one aircraft spotting a convoy of six ships and claiming a large steamer sunk. Repeatedly attacked by nightfighters during its return flight, the *Sparviero* managed to escape without damage. However, Tenente Alessandro Senni of 105° *Gruppo* failed to return from this mission.

Two days later eight S.79s from 105°, 130° and 132° *Gruppi Aerosiluranti* repeatedly attacked Convoy TE 14. One *Sparviero* was intercepted and damaged by a No 32 Sqn Hurricane IIC, the aircraft being forced to break off before dropping its torpedo. The seven remaining torpedo-bombers (four of which were flown by Capitani Giulio Cesare Graziani and Urbano Mancini, Tenente Giuseppe Cimicchi and Sottotenente Carlo Pfister) continued with their mission. At 1830 hrs these *Sparvieri* torpedoed and badly damaged the 1893-ton auxiliary anti-aircraft ship HMS *Pozarica,* which then took shelter in Bougie harbour. It capsized here on 13 February, becoming a total loss.

On 6 February, during an action off the Syrian coast, a three-strong S.79 patrol from 104° *Gruppo Aerosiluranti* (aircraft flown by Tenenti Enrico Marescalchi and Alberto Dattrino and Sottotenente Del Ponte) sighted the 75-ton Egyptian motorised sailing vessel *Al Ameriaah*. The ship was promptly strafed and sunk by the three *Aerosiluranti*. The next day three S.79 torpedo-bombers were badly damaged on Elmas airfield at 1505 hrs during a raid by 15 B-17 and B-26 bombers of the USAAF's Twelfth Air Force.

Another action occurred on 9 February when four 105° *Gruppo* and three 1° *Nucleo AS Sparvieri* attacked vessels off Algiers. 1° *Nucleo AS* ace Maggiore Erasi claimed a steamer hit in the harbour while Tenente Colonnello Carlo Unia attacked a nearby freighter, his action being met by heavy flak. Unia's co-pilot, Maresciallo Codognini, seeing his pilot closing dangerously on the target, and tracer converging on their aircraft, twisted in his seat and screamed excitedly, *'L'è matt, l'è matt!'* ('He's crazy, he's crazy'). Unia dropped his torpedo at a range of less than 1000 m (1100 yds), but the searchlights' dazzling beams and fierce flak did not allow him to observe the outcome of the attack.

Just prior to this engagement Maggiore Emilio Verrascina's S.79 had been intercepted by two fighters, but the aircraft had escaped with its torpedo still slung underneath.

On 28 February 132° *Gruppo Aerosiluranti* suffered a grave loss when Sottotenente Carlo Pfister lost his life along with all his crew, crashing in Sicily aboard an S.79 that they had just accepted from the *Squadra Riparazioni* (repair unit) at Palermo. Squadronmate Sottotenente Martino Aichner later recalled Pfister's last flight;

'There were low clouds, and Graziani, Pfister and I had to move three aircraft from Trapani to Catania. Graziani and I came in from the sea south of Syracuse, wary of running into barrage balloons raised to protect the harbour. Pfister wanted to cut through among the mountains. He had already completed the most difficult stage of the flight, tucking into the valleys among the fringes of the clouds. He had overflown Caltagirone, which was only a few tens of metres high, and just where the rich, green Lentini plain opened out a wing hit the ground and the aircraft literally crumpled up.'

New York-born Pfister was among the most distinguished torpedo-bomber pilots in the *Regia Aeronautica*, and for actions flown since September 1942 he received a posthumous Gold Medal for Military Valour.

LAST DAYLIGHT ATTACK

On 27 March an Allied convoy codenamed *Untrue* was sighted northwest of the Algerian port of Philippeville. Four three-strong S.79 patrols (two each from 105° and 89° *Gruppi*) duly took off from Decimomannu between 1010 and 1020 hrs with orders to attack the Allied vessels. The first three 105° *Gruppo* S.79s, led by Capitano Giulio Ricciarini, were intercepted by a pair of No 43 Sqn Spitfires and forced to break off. The second S.79 patrol, from 105° *Gruppo* and led by Capitano Urbano Mancini, was intercepted 25 miles north-northeast of Cape de Fer by another No 43 Sqn section, with tragic consequences. The two Spitfires downed all three S.79s, with Flg Off Anthony Snell claiming two (one of which was Mancini's) and Sgt Hermiston one.

Before his aircraft was shot down, Capitano Mancini torpedoed and sank the 9545-ton freighter *Empire Rowan*, and at 1220 hrs he radioed, 'Mission accomplished. I return'. His success was confirmed by 89° *Gruppo* crews who, overflying the area soon after the 105° *Gruppo* attack, saw a large ship burning. His last action, combined with his former command service, earned Mancini a posthumous Gold Medal for Military Valour.

At 1150 hrs the two S.79 patrols of 89° *Gruppo*, led respectively by Tenenti Irnerio Bertuzzi and Battista Mura, attacked the convoy, but without success. The formation lost two *Sparvieri*, one being downed by No 43 Sqn Spitfire V pilots Flg Offs Torrance and ace Robert Turkington. The second *Sparviero* was shared between No 323 Wing

Born in New York in 1915, Sottotenente Carlo Pfister lost his life when his S.79 crashed near Palermo on 28 February 1943. By then he had become one of the most distinguished pilots in the *Aerosiluranti*, having taken part in several actions with 132° *Gruppo*. The very active role Pfister played in combat from September 1942 earned him a well deserved posthumous *Medaglia d'Oro al Valor Militare* (*Aeronautica Militare*)

On 27 March 1943 Capitano Urbano Mancini, CO of 105° *Gruppo*, torpedoed and sank the freighter *Empire Rowan*, only to then be shot down and killed along with his crew by a No 43 Sqn Spitfire flown by Flg Off Anthony Snell. This sinking, and his former deeds, earned Mancini a posthumous *Medaglia d'Oro al Valor Militare* (*Aeronautica Militare*)

On 27 March 1943 Tenente Irnerio Bertuzzi of 89° *Gruppo* attacked the *Untrue* convoy, but to no avail. Following the armistice he joined the *Aeronautica Repubblicana*'s torpedo-bomber *Gruppo* 'Buscaglia' in the north. Post-war, he left the Italian Air Force to fly as a civilian pilot, later becoming the pilot for ENI (*Ente Nazionale Idrocarburi* – National Hydrocarbon Society) president Enrico Mattei. On 27 October 1962 both men and an American journalist lost their lives when their Morane-Saulnier aircraft exploded and crashed near Pavia, in northern Italy. A 2003 investigation by Pavia's public prosecutor concluded that the aircraft had been sabotaged (*Nino Arena*)

A 104° *Gruppo* serviceman paints the white silhouettes of British warships and merchantmen claimed by his unit on an aircraft. These alleged successes include a battleship and a carrier whose profile resembles that of *Argus* (*SME*)

CO Wg Cdr Michael Pedley, who was flying a Hurricane II, and the convoy's gunners.

These heavy losses marred the last large-scale daylight attack flown by Italian torpedo-bombers, which had already begun to operate under the cover of darkness. The next day (28 March) the *Regia Aeronautica* celebrated the 20th anniversary of its formation. At Pisa airport *il Duce* Benito Mussolini reviewed a line-up of 41° *Gruppo* S.79s equipped with new remotely-controlled torpedoes, which were destined never to be used in action.

Another significant disaster befell the *Aerosiluranti* on 5 April when four S.79s of 41° *Gruppo's* 205ª *Squadriglia*, led by Capitano Ernesto Brambilla, took off from Sardinia at 1805 hrs. For reasons that remain unknown, the entire formation failed to return. Five days later Capitano Vito Di Mola, CO of 131° *Gruppo's* 279ª *Squadriglia*, also failed to return – 131° *Gruppo* had been based at Gerbini, on Sicily, since 1 April, having replaced 132° *Gruppo*.

Altogether, from 27 March to 10 April the *Aerosiluranti* force had lost ten aircrews out of 25 engaged in action, and had sunk only the *Empire Rowan* in return. After these appalling losses many *Aerosiluranti* were shifted to Tuscany, where, in early June 1943, with 284ª *Squadriglia* and 108° *Gruppo* at Pisa-San Giusto and 204ª *Squadriglia* with 89° *Gruppo* at Siena-Ampugnano, the *Raggruppamento Aerosiluranti* (*Rgpt AS*) was formed. The new unit, covering the 3° *Squadra Aerea*, brought together 44 airworthy S.79s. It would be employed as a 'fire brigade' wherever its intervention was urgently required.

MAY-JUNE NIGHT ACTIONS

After the Axis surrender in Tunisia on 13 May, *Sparvieri* flew relentless operations from then until the end of June in an attempt to disrupt Allied forces as they prepared for the invasion of Sicily. On the night of 20/21 May a 131° *Gruppo* S.79 of 279ª *Squadriglia*, piloted by Tenente Fresta, attacked a convoy of 25 ships 25 miles northwest of Bone, but the aircraft was hit and set ablaze. Fresta dropped his torpedo despite the flames, and then the badly burned crew took to their dinghy after ditching. They were captured by a British ship later that night.

Between 0245 hrs and 0305 hrs on 23 May seven S.79s from 284ª *Squadriglia* and 89° and 131° *Gruppi* attacked shipping off the Algerian coast. At 0510 hrs one S.79 targeted a 5000-ton steamer in Bougie Bay, but the result of the attack could not be observed. That night four S.79s failed to return, ace Flg Off Peter Williamson in a Beaufighter VI of No 153 Sqn claiming two S.79s destroyed over the North African coast. Similar action occurred two nights later when four 36° *Stormo* S.79s made an offensive sweep at 0110 hrs on 25 May. Nightfighters chased two *Sparvieri* to no avail, but one S.79 failed to return. Ace Flt Lt Lieutenant Kenneth Rayment, again from No 153 Sqn, claimed an S.79 downed 45 miles northwest of Bone on the night of 23/24 May, so it is likely that there was a discrepancy in the dates given in Italian and British reports.

On 26 May three 104° *Gruppo* S.79s flown by Tenente Colonnello Ubaldo Puccio (the *gruppo*'s CO), Capitano Enrico Marescalchi and Tenente Alberto Dattrino attacked an escorted convoy 30 miles north of Mersa Matruh without success.

Operations continued throughout June. At 0130 hrs on the 24th, for example, four S.79s took off from Sardinia and were intercepted by a Beaufighter VI flown by Flt Lt Rayment. He duly shot down an S.79 over Djidjelli, this loss being confirmed by the Italians.

Between 0200 hrs and 0610 hrs on 25 June three S.79s flew an offensive sweep along the North African coast, and at 0350 hrs one of them attacked five ships anchored at Cape Cavallo, claiming a 7000-ton steamer hit. Again, an S.79 failed to return from this sortie, its loss being attributed to No 153 Sqn ace Flt Lt Laurence Styles. He claimed an S.79 55 miles north-northeast of Bougie on the night of 24/25 June. However, this claim could also relate to a *Reparto Speciale* S.79bis lost that same night.

OPERATION *SCOGLIO*

By early 1943 it was clear that Italy's fortunes in World War 2 were declining rapidly, and that an outstanding feat of arms was urgently needed to boost crumbling morale. Accordingly, in February, the *Regia Aeronautica* General Staff planned an air raid on Gibraltar – a target that was always useful for propaganda purposes.

For this raid, codenamed Operation *Scoglio* (Operation *Rock*, from the island's nickname), the Italians selected ten torpedo-bomber crews from

Five of the most skilful Italian torpedo-bomber aces were selected for the bold June 1943 raid against Gibraltar. They are, from left to right, Capitani Giulio Cesare Graziani and Francesco Di Bella, Maggiore Franco Melley and Capitani Marino Marini and Giuseppe Cimicchi (*Aeronautica Militare*)

The S.79bis was an improved *Sparviero* variant powered by Alfa Romeo 128 engines that was chosen to carry out Operation *Scoglio* – a daring night attack on Gibraltar – on 19/20 June 1943 (*Aeronautica Militare*)

the most effective anti-shipping force they had at their disposal in the Mediterranean. These handpicked aircrews, each led by a renowned ace pilot, formed a unit designated the *Reparto Speciale Aerosiluranti* (often quoted as *Gruppo Speciale Aerosiluranti*), which was set up specifically for this operation. The selected veteran pilots included Capitani Giuseppe Cimicchi, Giulio Cesare Graziani, Marino Marini, Carlo Faggioni, Francesco Di Bella, Dante Magagnoli, Giuseppe Amoruso, and Vittorio Pini and Maggiori Franco Melley and Gabriele Casini.

Led by the redoubtable Tenente Colonnello Carlo Unia, the new unit was equipped with the latest *Sparviero* variant, the S.79bis, which was faster and better armed than previous versions. To improve speed and range the S.79bis was fitted with the new Alfa Romeo 128 engines and had had its ventral gondola removed.

On 19 June the ten *Reparto Speciale* long-range S.79bis trimotors moved to Istres, in southern France, for the planned torpedo attack on Gibraltar. The undercarriage of the aircraft flown by Capitano Graziani and Tenente Porthos Ammannato collapsed on landing, rendering it useless. Therefore, at around midnight on the 20th, only nine torpedo-bombers took off for Gibraltar. However, seven were forced to turn back owing to mechanical problems, leaving just two aircraft, flown by torpedo aces Cimicchi and Faggioni, to attack the island.

The British were taken completely by surprise, their anti-aircraft batteries being unable to open fire and only their searchlights working. The two S.79bis dropped their torpedoes, Cimicchi expending his at 0510 hrs just as his aircraft was illuminated by a searchlight. He released his weapon at freighters anchored in the merchant vessel harbour near the Spanish town of La Linea. It is reported that Cimicchi dropped his torpedo from a range of 1500 m (1640 yds) at an altitude of 200 m (650 ft). Faggioni dropped at 0539 hrs after his torpedo release device had initially failed at 0516 hrs. Both crews disengaged successfully but their torpedoes failed to explode. Cimicchi returned to Istres at 0940 hrs, but Faggioni ran out of fuel and forced-landed near Barcelona, in Spain. His aircraft was interned and the aircrew were later repatriated. Despite its unsuccessful outcome, the Gibraltar raid was a remarkable action.

The *Reparto* Speciale's *Sparvieri* were back in action on the night of 24/25 June, making an anti-shipping sweep along the North African coast in the Bougie-Algiers-Oran sector. Eight S.79bis torpedo-bombers left Istres between 0200 hrs and 0220 hrs, but only five of them were able to launch torpedoes at as many freighters, and again to no avail. Tragically, the unit paid dearly for this disappointing result as Capitano Vittorio Pini's *Sparviero* failed to return, all of its crew being listed as missing.

On 27 June the *Reparto Speciale Aerosiluranti*, commanded by Tenente Colonnello Unia, returned to Littoria from Istres. Unfortunately, this return trip was marked by yet another loss when Tenente Pasquale Vinciguerra's S.79bis, carrying specialist groundcrewmen, crashed between Forlì and Ferrara in northern Italy due to poor weather, killing all on board.

IN THE DARKNESS OVER SICILY

On 9 July the Allies initiated Operation *Husky* when they landed on Sicily, the *Aerosiluranti* having started harassing the invasion convoys on the eve of the campaign.

At that time the S.79 torpedo-bomber force numbered 99 aircraft (41 airworthy), shared between 205ᵃ *Squadriglia* at Milis, Sardinia (four airworthy trimotors), 279ᵃ *Squadriglia* at Gerbini, Sicily (with four aircraft, but only one of which was airworthy), 104° *Gruppo* at Gadurra (11 aircraft, five airworthy), 130° *Gruppo* at Littoria (nine aircraft, two airworthy), 132° *Gruppo* at Gorizia (five aircraft, none airworthy), the *Rgpt AS* at Pisa and Siena (44 *Sparvieri*, 15 airworthy), 1° *Nucleo AS* at Gorizia (12 aircraft, six airworthy) and 3° *Nucleo AS* at Salon, in France (ten aircraft, eight airworthy). Two other units, 109° *Gruppo* at Pisa and 2° *Nucleo AS* at Naples-Capodichino, both had sufficient personnel for a section each, but no aircraft for them to fly.

At 2115 hrs on 7 July two 108° *Gruppo* S.79s flown by Tenenti Francesco Pandolfo (256ᵃ *Squadriglia*) and Bernardo Braghieri (257ᵃ *Squadriglia*) left Sardinia for an attacking sweep along the Tunisian coast. At 2245 hrs Braghieri, with Maresciallo Silvio Fiorentu as co-pilot, claimed a 7000-ton steamer stricken 20 miles southeast of Galite Island. Pandolfo, with co-pilot Sergente Maggiore Lorenzo Sciarra, claimed a 6000-ton steamer hit at 2250 hrs. The following night five S.79s were up from Sardinia, and they claimed strikes on four large steamers, two of which were reported as sunk.

During the night of 9/10 July the invasion of Sicily really got into its stride, and the first attacks on the Allied fleet were launched by *Rgpt AS* S.79s, but to no avail. Torpedo-bombers attacked the invasion fleet through the nights of 11 and 12 July also, the aircraft mostly involved being the *Sparvieri* from Sardinia and 3rd and 4th *Squadra Aerea*. The 4th *Squadra Aerea* bore the brunt of the losses, as three *Sparvieri* failed to return from attacks on Allied shipping east of Cape Passero and a fourth, flown by Tenente Egone Bucher, was forced to ditch after claiming to have hit a large cruiser.

Sicilian-born 'Ciccio' Di Bella, despite being troubled by wounds sustained on the Greek Front, rushed to defend his native island. He got the chance on the night of 11/12 July, when S.79s attacked the western side of invasion sector *Joss*. Although US Navy destroyers USS *Murphy* (DD 603) and USS *McLanahan* (DD 615) reported several near misses,

Sicilian-born torpedo-bomber ace Capitano Francesco Aurelio Di Bella, known to his squadronmates as 'Ciccio', damaged the cruiser HMS *Manchester* on 23 July 1941. He was among the few *Aerosiluranti* pilots awarded the *Medaglia d'Oro al Valor Militare* during their lifetime. In 1943 Di Bella fought to defend his native Sicily, and after the war he distinguished himself as a politician. He passed away in early April 1972 (*Aeronautica Militare*)

Di Bella and Tenente Luigi Buonaiuto launched their torpedoes at a steamer and a cruiser (both 10,000-ton), respectively. Neither pilot could observe the results of their attacks, however, because nightfighters were in the area.

That same night, at 2200 hrs, three 132° *Gruppo* S.79s from 278ª *Squadriglia*, flown by Capitani Faggioni and Valerio and Tenente Marino Marini, attacked a convoy of two steamers and five destroyers between Augusta and Cape Passero. Crews saw one large steamer ablaze after their torpedo runs. A short while later Tenenti Caio Tredici and Giuseppe Coci were unable to observe the result of a torpedo fired at a destroyer south of Augusta because of nightfighters.

Finally, an S.79 of the *Aeronautica Sardegna*, flown by Capitano Alberto Piacentino and *Generale di Brigata Aerea* Virgilio Sala (the *Rgpt AS* CO), attacked a 10,000-ton cruiser off Gela on the night of 12 July. The crew could not observe the result owing to heavy anti-aircraft fire, and their S.79 landed back in Sardinia at 0140 hrs.

On the night of 12/13 July an S.79 narrowly escaped attack by a nightfighter that pursued it until the aircraft had landed – that night Beaufighters of No 600 Sqn claimed six kills and one damaged. The next night, 13/14 July, 16 S.79s were in action, 3rd and 4th *Squadra Aerea* providing five and eleven aircraft, respectively. Among the latter, which started taking off from Lecce shortly after 2000 hrs, the 41° *Gruppo* S.79 flown by Tenente Raffaele Durante developed yaw on takeoff and crashed into a parked Z.1007bis, both aircraft going up in flames. Durante's crew escaped unscathed.

At 2250 hrs on the 13th all remaining S.79s attacked ships in Augusta Bay. Di Bella, with his faithful co-pilot Sergente Gambino, claimed a 10,000-ton steamer probably sunk, Capitano Carlo Faggioni of 132° *Gruppo*'s 278ª *Squadriglia* reported a destroyer sunk and Capitano Franco Prati claimed a 5000-ton cruiser hit. Tenente Ottone Sponza, Faggioni's wingman, aimed his weapon at a steamer but was unable to observe the result.

Among the S.79s that had taken off from Lecce were some from 104° *Gruppo*. Capitani Marescalchi and Romani, both of 253ª *Squadriglia*, launched torpedoes at ships south of Syracuse but the anti-aircraft barrage prevented them observing results. Both of the 104° *Gruppo* trimotors were intercepted and damaged by nightfighters but they returned to base. A third 253ª *Squadriglia* S.79, flown by Tenente Alberto Dattrino, attacked a steamer ten miles off Augusta but it was damaged by anti-aircraft fire, returning to base four hours later. Even Tenente Colonello Ubaldo Puccio, the 104° *Gruppo* CO, claimed one destroyer hit that night. Maggiore Massimiliano Erasi of 41° *Gruppo* and Capitano Alfredo Reyer of 104° *Gruppo*'s 252ª *Squadriglia* also claimed a 10,000-ton cruiser hit apiece. Reyer's S.79 was then intercepted over Lecce airfield by a nightfighter intruder whose bursts badly damaged the *Sparviero*'s tail unit. An S.79 of 41° 's *Gruppo*'s 204ª *Squadriglia*, flown by Tenente Luigi Buonaiuto, failed to return.

On the night of 14/15 July S.79s attacked warships off Cape Passero, launching torpedoes at the cruisers *Euryalus* and *Cleopatra* and two destroyers, all unsuccessfully.

After several disappointments, on 16 July the *Sparvieri* finally achieved a remarkable result. That night at 0025 hrs an S.79 from the *Rgpt AS* of the 4th *Squadra Aerea* (Apulia), flown by Capitano Carlo Capelli and Tenente Ennio Caselli, launched a torpedo at a significant prey – the 26,812-ton carrier HMS *Indomitable*, which had been caught by the *Sparviero* 40 miles south of Cape Passero. The torpedo struck the carrier's port side, flooding its boiler hold and killing seven sailors. Capelli's S.79 disengaged without damage, and the carrier took shelter in Malta at 0730 hrs on 17 July, sailing at 11 knots. After initial repairs *Indomitable* left at 14 knots for Gibraltar, which it reached safely. The vessel later underwent extensive repairs in Great Britain.

On that night eight *Sparvieri* had attacked ships between Capes Passero and Murro di Porco ('Pig's Snout') to no avail, apart from the *Indomitable* episode. The attackers included, as usual, Capitano Di Bella (always supported by Sergente Gambino), who was credited with hitting an 8000/10,000-ton steamer near Augusta. The next night's raids, flown by nine S.79s, saw no losses, but things were to be different on 17/18 July when six S.79s were sent to attack ships in the Augusta area. Di Bella claimed a 12,000-ton steamer, which, according to Italian reports, exploded because it was laden with ammunition.

Before and after this action Di Bella's *Sparviero* was repeatedly attacked by nightfighters and, as if that was not enough, it was also hit by naval anti-aircraft fire. The S.79 began burning, and with fuel leaking from riddled tanks, its engines started running roughly too, Di Bella decided ditching was the best option, as a worsening of the fire could have caused the aircraft to explode. The ditching, near Cape Vaticano, Calabria, was successful, the bomber's crew sustaining only minor injuries. They were

Some very relieved and satisfied aircrew from 41° *Gruppo*'s 204ª *Squadriglia* just back from a mission. At the beginning of June 1943 204ª *Squadriglia* was among units forming the *Raggruppamento Aerosiluranti*, destined to operate over the Tyrrhenian Sea and Sicily. Because of the Allied mastery of the skies the *Raggruppamento* flew nightly, with its S.79s painted in dark schemes overall. On 16 July 1943 the British carrier HMS *Indomitable* was torpedoed and seriously damaged south of Cape Passero by an S.79 of the *Raggruppamento* – a prestigious prey for the *Sparvieri* (*SME*)

picked up a few hours later by a German S-Boat, which ferried them safely to Naples harbour.

The relentless actions he flew over the waters of his native Sicily in July 1943 earned Capitano Francesco Aurelio Di Bella the *Medaglia d'Oro al Valor Militare*. Once again, remarkably, this award had been bestowed upon a living airman at a time when Gold Medals were mostly awarded posthumously.

On 18/19 July the *Regia Aeronautica* sent five 3rd and 4th *Squadra Aerea* S.79s up over Augusta. Two of these aircraft, from 253ª *Squadriglia* (Capitano Enrico Marescalchi and Tenente Ferruccio Coloni) took off from Lecce and attacked warships shelling the coast between Syracuse and Augusta. Marescalchi escaped a nightfighter attack and returned to base with his machine badly holed, but Coloni's S.79 was so badly shot up that it had to be ditched off Calabria. After two days in their raft Coloni's exhausted crew reached the Calabrian shore near Riace Marina, later returning to their unit.

On the night of the 19/20 July two 130° *Gruppo* S.79s left Littoria airfield. After evading a nightfighter, one of them dropped its torpedo at a 4000/5000-ton freighter ten miles offshore between Capes Murro di Porco and Passero at 0250 hrs. The other *Sparviero* returned to base with its torpedo still attached.

The following night two 130° *Gruppo* S.79s attacked a convoy of six freighters off Syracuse, reporting one torpedo hit on a steamer that was seen to blow up. An S.79 failed to return from this action. On 21/22 July *Sparvieri* made several torpedo attacks in the Cape Passero–Augusta sector, but failed to score.

Almost three weeks later, the *Regia Aeronautica* sent three *Sparvieri* against a convoy detected south of Catania on 9 August, the Italians reporting a 5000-ton freighter hit and two others as 'probables'.

August 1943 would see the death of yet another prominent torpedo-bomber pilot. Having seen considerable action up to December 1942, Tenente Colonnello Vittorio Cannaviello was posted to the *Regia Aeronautica* staff. He remained here through the spring of 1943, when, as a reward for his work, he was sent to eastern Europe as an air attaché. But this prestigious posting, which might have been desired by many, did not satisfy Cannaviello. The ever-worsening position that Italy found itself in in the Mediterranean made him anxious to get back into action. The invasion of Sicily was the final straw, and he officially asked his senior officers in Rome to return him to active duty. This was authorised, and at the beginning of August Cannaviello was posted to 132° *Gruppo Autonomo Aerosiluranti*, based at Littoria (now Latina) near Rome.

On the night of 12 August Cannaviello took off from Littoria, leading three S.79s of 132° *Gruppo* in an attack on a convoy sighted between Palermo, Trapani and the Sicilian Channel. Weather conditions were poor, and for unknown reasons the three *Sparvieri* failed to return. Whether they were downed by enemy defences or poor weather was never ascertained. Having relinquished the safety of diplomatic immunity in order to defend his country, Cannaviello was posthumously awarded a well-deserved *Medaglia d'Oro al Valor Militare*.

This courageous officer was subsequently avenged by 132° *Gruppo*'s torpedo airmen, who scored a succession of ship 'kills' during several

Tenente Colonnello Vittorio Cannaviello rightfully ranked among the most respected Italian torpedo-bomber commanders, leading 34° *Gruppo* in 1941 and 2° *Nucleo AS* from 8 August that year. Despite being appointed an air attaché, he chose to resume active service with 132° *Gruppo*. Sadly, on 12 August 1943, he failed to return from a sortie over Sicilian waters. For his devotion to duty he received a well deserved but sadly posthumous *Medaglia d'Oro al Valor Militare* (*Aeronautica Militare*)

single-handed actions flown from Sardinia – six S.79s had been deployed on the island since mid-August. Over the nights of 15 and 16 August the Sardinian-based trimotors sank, near Cani Island (Bizerte), the British 2750-ton Tank Landing Ship LST-414 (credited to Capitano Carlo Faggioni) and, ten miles off Cape Bougaroun, the 2700-ton steamer *Empire Kestrel* (attacked by Capitano Giuseppe Cimicchi). Also on the night of 16 August, the US 7126-ton freighter *Benjamin Contee*, sailing from Bone harbour for Oran with 1800 Italian PoWs on board, was torpedoed and damaged by Tenente Vezio Terzi 16 miles north of Cape de Garde. The US freighter was so badly damaged that it was withdrawn from service, being used in June 1944 as an element of one of the famous Mulberry Harbours following the D-Day landings at Normandy.

Shortly after his attack on the *Benjamin Contee*, veteran torpedo-bomber pilot Capitano Giuseppe Cimicchi was awarded the *Medaglia d'Oro al Valor Militare* for his courageous actions between 1941 and 1943.

The night of 15 August also saw 24 S.79s of 41°, 108° and 131° *Gruppi* in action. All of them attacked shipping in Sicilian waters, but Tenente Tabacco's aircraft failed to return.

On the night of 7 September the *Regia Aeronautica* carried out attacks against Allied shipping north of Sicily. During one of these raids, an S.79 of the 132° *Gruppo*, flown by Tenente Vasco Pagliarusco, torpedoed the 1625-ton British vessel LST-417, forcing it to run aground on the shore near Termini Imerese. This was the *Aerosiluranti's* last success before the armistice that was announced on 8 September.

Other *Sparvieri* were also airborne in the hours leading up to the Italian armistice. Indeed, late in the afternoon of the 8th, 12 S.79s took off from Pisa and Siena to attack Allied vessels that had been detected approaching

One of 132° *Gruppo's* last victories was scored by Capitano Giuseppe Cimicchi when he sank the steamer *Empire Kestrel* off Cape Bougaroun on 16 August 1943. The relentless actions he flew during the war earned him the *Medaglia d'Oro al Valor Militare* while he was still alive. This courageous pilot, also awarded four *Medaglie d'Argento*, three *Medaglie di Bronzo*, one *Croce di Guerra al Valor Militare* and a German Iron Cross 2nd Class, passed away on 15 October 1992 (*via author*)

the Gulf of Salerno. Although eight were subsequently ordered back to base by 3rd *Squadra Aerea* Command, four pressed on and attacked the ships, but without result. Among the machines called back were two S.79s from 104° *Gruppo*, flown by Capitani Alfredo Reyer and Enrico Marescalchi (the COs of 252ª and 253ª *Squadriglie*, respectively) after they had taken off at 1940 hrs.

Then came the drama following the armistice of 8 September 1943, involving *Gruppi Aerosiluranti* and many other Italian military units alike. At Siena-Ampugnano airport 104° *Gruppo* (252ª and 253ª *Squadriglie*) had 12 *Sparvieri* (eight airworthy), while nine others (six airworthy) were with 132° *Gruppo* (278ª and 281ª *Squadriglie*) at Littoria. The 41°, 108° and 131° *Gruppi* sub-units of the *Rgpt AS*, based at Siena-Ampugnano and Pisa-San Giusto, had serviceable strengths of 13, three and six *Sparvieri*, respectively.

On 10 September ten 132° *Gruppo* S.79s and two S.82s left Littoria before the Germans arrived and flew to Siena-Ampugnano. The *Sparvieri* deployed at Pisa-San Giusto were captured by the Germans, however.

News of the armistice surprised Capitano Carlo Faggioni, who was on leave in his hometown, Carrara. Towards the end of August 1943 this brave officer had shown signs of a nervous breakdown, and needed a short rest period. Hearing of the armistice, Faggioni immediately tried to reach Littoria, but the train he was aboard stopped at Cerveteri, north of Rome. Undeterred, the indomitable officer got off and began marching along the Aurelian Route. Suddenly, he realised he was close to Cerveteri airfield, and some of its *Sparvieri* were parked on the runway. Faggioni approached the trimotors and boarded one that, luckily, was already refuelled. He took off and flew to Littoria, where he assumed command of 278ª *Squadriglia*. As already mentioned, on 10 September 132° *Gruppo Sparvieri*, including Faggioni's, left Littoria for Siena-Ampugnano.

On the morning of 11 September the 3rd *Squadra Aerea* Command ordered that all 28 S.79s deployed at Siena-Ampugnano be flown south to Sardinian bases. Of the airborne *Sparvieri* from 104°, 132° and 41° *Gruppi*, at least 13 landed successfully at Decimomannu and six more at Milis (the crews of these latter machines were initially captured by the Germans and then released). One 204ª *Squadriglia* S.79 (flown by Sottotenente Corbellini) ditched near Ustica. Only the flight engineer survived, being rescued by fishermen. A 205ª *Squadriglia Sparviero* headed north.

Four unfortunate S.79s from 132° *Gruppo*'s 278ª *Squadriglia* were intercepted near La Maddalena by Bf 109Gs of JG 77. According to some sources this one-sided combat between former allies resulted in Oberleutnant Wolfgang Ernst of *Staffel* 9./JG 77 claiming three victories – one Z.1007 and two 'Breda 88s', shot down at 1032 hrs, 1033 hrs and 1040 hrs, respectively. Despite the Z.1007 claimed by Ernst, the Italians reported just two Cants downed by German flak. The 'Breda 88s' were two S.79 trimotors flown by Tenente Ottone Sponza and Sottotenente Giuseppe Coci. The surviving *Sparvieri,* piloted by Capitano Carlo Faggioni and Tenente Leopoldo Ruggeri, had to return to Siena-Ampugnano.

An S.79 of 104° *Gruppo*'s 252ª *Squadriglia*, flown by Tenente Nannini, also landed there, it too having been intercepted off the Tuscan coast by JG 77's Bf 109Gs and forced to turn back.

Two S.79s of 41° *Gruppo*'s 204ª *Squadriglia*, flown by Tenenti Crespi and Balboni, landed safely at Gerbini, in Sicily (some sources reported that a third S.79 flown by Tenente Boccioli landing there too). There, they were joined by three other *Sparvieri* that had taken off singly – one from Fano (flown by Capitano Giulio Cesare Graziani), one from Foligno (flown by Capitano 'Ciccio' Di Bella) and the third from Malpensa, near Milan (flown by Tenente Simoni).

Altogether, 34 *Sparvieri* had set off for Allied-controlled territory. Of these, 28 came from Siena-Ampugnano, one from Foligno, one from Malpensa, one from Fano, two from Guidonia and one from Rome-Littorio. Ten were lost. One reached northern Italy, another ditched near Ustica Island, two were downed by German fighters, three were intercepted by German fighters and forced back to Siena and three were disabled in accidents. Thus, only 24 of the escaping *Sparvieri* remained serviceable.

'Ciccio' Di Bella cooperated closely with the Allies and was then discharged in July 1944. Even the post-war era proved successful for the Sicilian ace, who married and was elected a deputy in the Parliament of the Italian Republic. After a full and adventurous life Francesco Aurelio Di Bella passed away in early April 1972 at Grosseto, in Tuscany, where he had retired.

Giulio Cesare Graziani joined the ICAF, again assuming command of 132° *Gruppo*'s 281ª *Squadriglia*. In July 1944 this *gruppo*, led by Maggiore Massimiliano Erasi, became part of *Stormo Baltimore*, equipped with Baltimore twin-engined bombers. From November 1944, as part of the Balkan Air Force, the *Stormo Baltimore* began hammering German targets in the Balkans. When Maggiore Erasi fell in combat on 21 February 1945, Graziani once again assumed temporary command of 132° *Gruppo*, ending the war with 78 sorties to his credit (20 November 1944 to 5 May 1945). He was then involved in important changes in the post-war *Aeronautica Militare*, reaching the rank of general. After being discharged Graziani maintained an active role in the Italian Air Force veteran associations, passing away on 23 December 1998. Evidence of his courage was provided by one Gold, six Silver and one Bronze Medal, three War Crosses for Military Valour and one Iron Cross 2nd Class.

On 13 September 1943 the 13 *Sparvieri* deployed at Decimomannu left Sardinia, Sicily-bound, but on landing at Castelvetrano two 253ª *Squadriglia* S.79s swung disastrously and were disabled. The first accident, involving Tenente Alberto Dattrino's aircraft, was caused by the tension of the moment. The second crash was due to the aircraft's two pilots, Tenenti Caio Tredici and Guido Riparbelli, showing off. The latter yelled in roman dialect to his companion, '*A Caio, faje vedè come ce sapemo fà!*' ('Hey Caio, show them what we can do!'). Accordingly, the S.79 made several reckless turns and ground-level passes, which ended with a disastrous yawing crash into two American aircraft. One of the two 41° *Gruppo* S.79s that landed at Gerbini on the 11th met the same fate, this time at the hands of an American test pilot. With this latter loss, S.79 write-offs totalled three.

The *Sparvieri* stood at Castelvetrano from 13 to 15 September, then moved to Agrigento airfield. The S.79s left Agrigento on the 22nd with an escort of P-38 Lightning fighters provided by the 1st Fighter Group, all bound for Korba airfield, in Tunisia. Other S.79s also landed there,

Maggiore Massimiliano Erasi joined the ICAF as CO of 132° *Gruppo* after the Italian armistice, the unit being equipped with Baltimore bombers. His skill at hitting difficult ground targets, especially bridges, earned him the nickname of 'Mr Bridge'. Erasi was killed in action on 21 February 1945 while leading his *gruppo* against a target in Istria, and was posthumously awarded the *Medaglia d'Oro al Valor Militare* (*Aeronautica Militare*)

S.79s of the ICAF on Lecce-Galatina airfield in Apulia. The Allies principally used the *Sparvieri* in the transport role (*Aeronautica Militare*)

Seen here in a post-war photo, Capitano Giulio Cesare Graziani took off from Fano on 13 September 1943 and flew his *Sparviero* to Allied territory. He resumed fighting in ICAF Baltimores, leading 281ª *Squadriglia* and 132° *Gruppo* after Maggiore Erasi's loss. Following the conflict Graziani rose to senior rank in the *Aeronautica Militare*. In addition to the *Medaglia d'Oro al Valor Militare*, he was awarded six Silver Medals, one Bronze Medal and three War Crosses for Military Valour, plus an Iron Cross 2nd Class. Graziani passed away on 23 December 1998 (*Aeronautica Militare*)

bringing the total number of *Sparvieri* deployed on this Tunisian airfield to 15. The trimotors left Korba on 1 October and returned to Italy, moving to Apulian Lecce-Galatina airfield.

On 13 October 1943 the co-belligerent southern Italian government officially declared war on Germany. At the end of the month ICAF *Raggruppamento Bombardamento e Trasporti* strength included 16 *Sparvieri* with 132° *Gruppo* (which had been converted to the transport role, with 253ª and 281ª *Squadriglie* as S.79 sub-units) based at Apulian Leverano airfield. Some S.79s (five or six, according to different sources) were based at Sardinian Milis until 18 January 1944, when they were also transferred to 132° *Gruppo Trasporti*. Finally, other S.79s were operated by 2ª *Squadriglia* of 1° *Gruppo Trasporti*.

After the plan to form a bombardment *Stormo* with all available S.79s was abandoned, the last three months of 1943 saw *Sparvieri* used to drop leaflets on German-occupied central and northern Italy. Other S.79s were flown by 2° *Gruppo Trasporti* (102ª and 103ª *Squadriglie*), which had formed on 18 November 1943. In January 1944 there were 22 (15 airworthy) *Sparvieri* assigned to the *Regia Aeronautica*'s *Raggruppamento Bombardamento e Trasporti* (*BeT*), serving with 132° *Gruppo Trasporti* (253ª and 281ª *Squadriglie*) at Lecce.

On 1 July 1944 the co-belligerent *Sparvieri* were all reunited in the *Raggruppamento BeT*'s 3rd *Stormo Trasporti*. At least 21 (14 airworthy) equipped 240ª *Squadriglia* of 98° *Gruppo Trasporti* at Lecce. These *Sparvieri* flew either operational liaison flights or as military air couriers, firstly based at Lecce and then at Roma-Centocelle from December 1944. By early 1945 the *Stormo Trasporti* had 14 S.79s, of which ten were serviceable, in 240ª *Squadriglia* of 98° *Gruppo Trasporti* at Roma-Centocelle airport. When the war in Europe ended on 8 May 1945, 98° *Gruppo* had a strength of 21 *Sparvieri* (14 serviceable), and three others served with the *Squadriglia Autonoma Unità Aerea* (Air Unit Autonomous Flight). Surviving *Sparvieri* entered post-war service with the *Aeronautica Militare*, being used in training, transport and liaison roles until they were discarded in 1953.

SPARVIERI TO THE NORTH

Italians who chose to continue fighting alongside Germany after the September 1943 armistice joined the *Repubblica Sociale Italiana* (RSI), in northern Italy, which was created towards the end of the month. Between the autumn and winter of that year the RSI organised its own air force, the *Aeronautica Repubblicana* (AR, redesignated the *Aeronautica Nazionale Repubblicana* (ANR) on 29 June 1944).

Thanks to the intervention of Tenente Colonnello Remo Cadringher, former 105° *Gruppo* CO, the torpedo-bomber role was reconstituted within the AR. Cadringher appointed torpedo-bomber ace Tenente Colonnello Arduino Buri as Inspector of the *Aerosiluranti* branch. The operational flying unit was designated 1° *Gruppo Aerosiluranti* 'Buscaglia', its CO being Capitano Carlo Faggioni, formerly of 132° *Gruppo*. Initially, in October 1943, the *gruppo* had only one S.79 on charge, but by March 1944 it could muster an operational complement of 27 trimotors at Venegono and Gorizia airfields, where the *gruppo* was trained before entering action.

During that same October an S.79 in flight from Foligno to Gorizia was hijacked by Sottotenente Carlo Alberto De Felici and flown to Allied-held territory. Over Apulia, the pilot, Maresciallo Giovanni Riso, tried to make a wheels-up landing to render his *Sparviero* unserviceable, but the hijacker shot him instantly. The S.79 belly-landed hard near Molfetta and was badly damaged. British servicemen quickly helped the mortally wounded pilot, who died in hospital on 22 October. Following the hijacking De Felici undertook intelligence duties, and he was killed in a flying accident five years later.

On 15 November 1943, in the first tragic accident to befall the AR, an S.79 flown by Tenente Ettore Donati crashed near Piacenza in poor weather, killing all on board.

The *gruppo* was officially formed on 1 January 1944 at Venegono airfield, and on 9 February all personnel swore an oath of loyalty to the RSI in the presence of Capitano Faggioni and Tenente Colonnello Buri. The *Gruppo* 'Buscaglia' was subdivided into 1ª, 2ª and 3ª *Squadriglie*, led by Capitano Giuseppe Valerio, Tenente Irnerio Bertuzzi and Capitano Carlo Chinca, respectively, plus one *Squadriglia Complementare* for training (commanded by Capitano Dante Magagnoli). During early March the squadrons were tasked with attacking Allied shipping in the Mediterranean. Two support groups were moved to Gorizia and Perugia-Sant'Egidio airfields at this time too, the latter being an advanced landing ground (ALG) from which to attack the Allies' Anzio beachhead.

After the armistice Capitano Carlo Faggioni became the first CO of the *Aeronautica Repubblicana*'s torpedo-bomber *Gruppo* 'Buscaglia'. He was subsequently killed in action on 10 April 1944 while attacking Allied shipping in Anzio Bay. Capitano Marino Marini duly took his place as the unit's new commanding officer. Later, after it became known that Maggiore Buscaglia had fought on the Allied side, the *gruppo* was renamed 'Faggioni'. Faggioni's wartime awards included at least five *Medaglie d'Argento*, three *Medaglie di Bronzo al Valor Militare* and one Iron Cross 2nd Class. The RSI also awarded him a posthumous *Medaglia d'Oro al Valor Militare*, although this was not officially recognised by the post-war Italian Republic (*Nino Arena*)

The first sortie over Anzio Bay was flown on the night of 10 March by six S.79s (five from 2ª *Squadriglia* and one *gruppo* HQ), which dropped torpedoes from 18 m (60 ft). The Italians claimed three hits scored on several 7000-ton steamers, but Allied reports failed to confirm these strikes. An S.79 flown by Tenente Giovanni Teta failed to return from this raid, the Italians recording that it was shot down by nightfighters. After this action the *gruppo* had just 15 torpedoes left. The next day S.79bis B2-03, flown by Sottotenente Salvatore Galante, was returning from Perugia airfield to Gorizia when it disappeared after overflying Forlì, the entire crew being lost. Some sources suggested it was probably shot down over the Adriatic by British fighters.

Gruppo 'Buscaglia' personnel officially swore an oath of loyalty to the RSI on 9 February 1944. Here, Capitano Faggioni is presenting the unit's battle flag to flag-bearer Sottotenente Ugo Cusmano. The latter officer was to fall in combat with P-47s of the 57th FG on 6 April 1944. On the extreme left is *Aerosiluranti* Inspector Tenente Colonnello Arduino Buri (*Aeronautica Militare*)

On the 13th six of the *gruppo*'s S.79-IIIs were ordered to attack Anzio again, the aircraft initially being sent to the Perugia-Sant'Egidio ALG. There, S.79 B2-08, piloted by Tenente Giuseppe Balzarotti, was forced to return to Gorizia to replace its malfunctioning torpedo. Tragically, during the return flight the *Sparviero* was intercepted off Rimini by RAF Spitfires and destroyed, all of its crew being killed.

Thus, the attack on vessels in Anzio Bay was carried out by the five surviving S.79-IIIs, led by Capitano Faggioni, between 0100 hrs and 0140 hrs on 14 March. Due to fierce anti-aircraft fire the Italians were unable to observe the results of their launches, but another tragedy struck the *gruppo*. Turning sharply to avoid enemy fire, Tenente Francesco Pandolfo's B1-02 lost wireless operator 1° Aviere Renzo Signorini, who was hurled out of the S.79 into the sea.

Gruppo 'Buscaglia's' troubles continued on 18 March when Gorizia was targeted by B-24 Liberators of the USAAF's Fifteenth Air Force. S.79bis B2-02 was destroyed and three other *Sparvieri* damaged. After this raid Capitano Faggioni decided to shift the *gruppo* to Lonate Pozzolo airfield, near Varese. This was completed by 2 April, and attack sorties resumed from this new base. However, disasters continued to befall the men of *Gruppo* 'Buscaglia'.

On 6 April 13 S.79-IIIs took off from Lonate Pozzolo to move to the ALG at Perugia. *Sparviero* B2-05, flown by Sottotenente De Lieto, turned back due to engine trouble. When they were over the Valdarno, near Montevarchi in Tuscany, the 12 remaining *Sparvieri* were jumped by four P-47 Thunderbolts of the USAAF's 64th FS/57th FG. The American fighters were flown by Maj C A Chamberlain, Capt Louis Frank and Lts R K Nevett and J J Lenihan. They massacred the S.79-IIIs, shooting down the four aircraft flown by Capitano Giulio Cesare Albini (B1-03), Sottotenente Ugo Cusmano (B1-07), Maresciallo Vittorio Daverio (B1-10) and Sergente Maggiore Giuseppe Fabbri (B2-55) in just a few minutes, with no survivors.

Among Albini's crew was Sergente Maggiore Nicola Gaeta, a decorated veteran of 281ª *Squadriglia* in the Aegean who, despite having a leg amputated following a raid on Cyprus on 4 July 1941, had resumed active service.

Two other *Sparvieri*, B1-33 (Sottotenente Marcello Perina) and B2-04 (Tenente Ottone Sponza), were badly shot up by Frank, Chamberlain and Nevett and made emergency landings. Altogether, following this bloody encounter, the *gruppo* had suffered at least 27 fatalities among officers, NCOs and specialists.

Despite this severe blow Capitano Faggioni did not lose heart, telling his men, 'It's hard, I know, but as long as I can I shall continue this way'. Accordingly, he stubbornly decided to lead five S.79-IIIs in an attack on Allied shipping in Anzio Bay. During the evening of 10 April four *Sparvieri* left Perugia (the fifth was damaged on takeoff), reaching their target area as planned. However, the fierce naval barrage the S.79s encountered caused severe losses. Faggioni's aircraft was shot down, killing the Italian ace and his crew, and the trimotor flown by Tenente Ottone Sponza was forced to ditch in flames. While trying to return to base, Capitano Giuseppe Valerio's S.79bis ran into a storm over the Apennines, crashing near Medesano, in Parma. The sole survivor was co-pilot Maresciallo Jasinski, who bailed out seriously wounded. Only the aircraft flown by Tenente Irnerio Bertuzzi escaped the slaughter, returning safely to Lonate Pozzolo.

Three days later Sottotenente Guerra's S.79bis crashed during a training flight, killing all on board. The *gruppo* was now decimated, and urgently needed a period of rest and reorganisation. On 12 April AR undersecretary Generale Arrigo Tessari and Tenente Colonnello Mario Bonzano visited Venegono airfield. That same afternoon Tessari presented the survivors of *Gruppo* 'Buscaglia' with money prizes, and assisted in the ceremony in which Tenente Irnerio Bertuzzi and his crew were awarded the Iron Cross 2nd Class.

Faggioni's loss had badly affected his men, and on 15 April another torpedo-bomber ace, Capitano Marino Marini, assumed command of *Gruppo* 'Buscaglia'. As of 31 May the *Gruppo* 'Buscaglia' had a strength of 28 S.79s (21 serviceable). That same day the *Squadriglia Complementare* was disbanded, its training duties being taken on by the *Squadriglia Scuola Aerosiluranti* at Venegono (led by Capitano Dante Magagnoli) and the *Squadriglia Addestramento Aerosiluranti* at Bettola (commanded by Capitano Michele Palumbo). The two new units came under the control of the *Comando Aerosiluranti* (led by Tenente Colonnello Arduino Buri), based at Venegono.

During March and April 1944 the *Gruppo* 'Buscaglia' had deployed 15 trimotors in action against the Anzio beachhead, taking off from the advanced airfield at Perugia-Sant'Egidio. Despite over-optimistic claims made by the aircrews involved, they achieved not one success, and paid a heavy toll in lives and aircraft that forced the unit to suspend all attacks. During May 1944 the *gruppo* underwent a much-needed rest and re-equipment period.

OVER GIBRALTAR AGAIN

During June 1944, thanks to the intense reorganisation undertaken by Capitano Marino Marini, the *Gruppo* 'Buscaglia' was made combat ready again. Both to underline its resumed will to fight and for propaganda purposes, a prestigious target was chosen – the Rock of Gibraltar.

A 1° *Gruppo* S.79bis is ready for takeoff under the watchful eyes of the unit's groundcrew (*Nino Arena*)

On 3 June, after taking off from Lonate Pozzolo at 0520 hrs, Capitano Marini led 12 *Sparvieri* to the springboard airfield at Istres, in southern France. From there ten *Aerosiluranti* took off at 2134 hrs the following day. The other two S.79s (Tenente Ruggeri's B3-09 and Tenente Abbate's B2-07) stayed in reserve. At the controls of the ten raiders were Capitani Marino Marini (B1-00), Irnerio Bertuzzi (B2-05) and Carlo Chinca (B3-04), Tenenti Francesco Pandolfo (B1-02), Vito Tornese (B3-07), Adriano Merani (B2-03) and Franco Monaco (B3-02) and Sottotenenti Domenico De Lieto (B2-09), Luigi Morselli (B3-03) and Francesco Del Prete (B2-10).

The first setback occurred when a mechanical failure forced Tenente Merani to turn back. He and his crew took off again aboard reserve trimotor B3-09, but this too suffered problems, compelling Merani to land on the airstrip at Perpignan. The other *Sparvieri* approached the target separately, Bertuzzi's S.79 reaching it first at 0220 hrs on 5 June. Moonlight fully illuminated the Rock, and the defences were taken by surprise, opening fire very late. Meanwhile, three British aircraft scrambled, two Swordfish and one Beaufighter. These failed to intercept the Italian raiders apart from the S.79 of Capitano Marini, who quickly left his pursuer behind.

Unfortunately, the Italian aircraft suffered more problems while attacking ships anchored in the roadstead. Owing to faulty release devices, some *Sparvieri* dropped their torpedoes only on their second attempt. Sottotenente De Lieto made two passes and was then forced to give up. The other aircrews claimed at least four freighters hit, although in reality their weapons had been stopped by anti-torpedo net barrages.

83

One struck a quay, injuring five men, this being the only actual 'success' for the mission. In addition, the harbour was closed for 12 hours after the Italian raid.

All S.79-IIIs made the return trip home with their central engine switched off so as to save fuel. Nevertheless, three aircraft, flown by Tenenti Monaco and Tornese and Sottotenente De Lieto, almost ran out of fuel and were forced to land in Spanish territory.

Among the other participating *Sparvieri*, two, flown by Capitano Marini and Sottotenente Del Prete, landed at Perpignan, while the remaining four (Bertuzzi, Morselli, Pandolfo and Chinca) landed at Istres at around 0734 hrs on 5 June. As expected, the Gibraltar raid was fully exploited by the fascist propaganda machine. Several Italian and German awards were presented to all aircrews in the shape of Silver Medals for Military Valour, while Capitano Marini was decorated with German Iron Crosses 1st and 2nd Classes. Bertuzzi and his crew were also awarded the Iron Cross 1st Class, while Tenente Pandolfo and Capitano Chinca, with their crews, received the Iron Cross, 2nd Class.

In the wake of the euphoria following the Gibraltar raid, Capitano Marini prepared another *Aerosiluranti* attack, this time targeting Bari harbour in southern Italy – a vital naval base for Allied military operations. On 6 July 1944 five S.79-IIIs of 2ª *Squadriglia* took off from Treviso at 0010 hrs, and at 0245 hrs they attacked enemy shipping anchored in the Apulian harbour. Aircrews of 1° *Gruppo Aerosiluranti* claimed a destroyer struck by Tenente Perina in B2-09, plus two ships sunk (one by Tenente Ruggeri's B2-12). A freighter was also reportedly torpedoed, but yet again the Allies failed to confirm any of these possible hits. The anti-aircraft batteries defending the harbour damaged *Sparviero* B2-10, forcing it to ditch off Ancona at 0420 hrs.

That July the *Gruppo* 'Buscaglia' reported a strength of about 20 aircraft, now ready for missions beyond Italian waters. This conviction was strengthened by the alleged successes claimed by the *Sparvieri* over Bari.

Aiming to attack Allied convoys in the Aegean Sea, ten S.79-IIIs from 1ª, 2ª and 3ª *Squadriglie* took off at 0545 hrs on 7 July, heading for Greece. After losing three aircraft (one temporarily) due to mechanical problems, and following two stopovers in Belgrade and Salonika, the seven remaining trimotors landed at Eleusis in the late afternoon of 8 July. The S.79s had no successes during the operations flown on 10 and 12 July. However, two aircraft, piloted by Capitano Chinca (B3-04) and Tenente Monaco (B3-02), were forced to ditch on the 12th after running out of fuel. The crews were saved by a German rescue seaplane. Following these losses the six remaining *Sparvieri* returned to Italy unscathed on 13-14 July, despite having to fly through appalling weather.

Some of the airmen from 1° *Gruppo* that took part in the daring Gibraltar raid on 5 June 1944. They are, from left to right, Sottotenente Marcello Perina (Sottotenente Del Prete's co-pilot), Tenenti Adriano Merani and Leopoldo Ruggeri, Aspirante Sottotenente Alfredo Bellucci (Capitano Bertuzzi's co-pilot), Capitano Irnerio Bertuzzi, Sottotenente Domenico De Lieto and Medical Tenente Lombardo. For this action Capitano Bertuzzi and his crew received both the Silver Medal for Military Valour and the German Iron Cross 1st Class (*Nino Arena*)

The *gruppo* spent some time at Lonate Pozzolo, hoping to reorganise for a second operational tour in the Aegean, but other setbacks occurred during this period. For example, on 29 July four S.79s were destroyed on the ground when Lonate was heavily strafed by Allied aircraft. Nevertheless, on 30 July six S.79-IIIs of 2ª *Squadriglia* took off in dreadful weather, ready for another operational tour in the eastern Mediterranean. During the transfer flight to Belgrade-Semlin, however, B2-04, flown by Tenente Neri, crashed on landing at Villafranca. The next day another eight *Sparvieri* joined them there, while two S.79-IIIs continued their flight to Belgrade.

At 0700 hrs that same day (31 July), four No 213 Sqn Mustang IIIs intercepted S.79bis B1-00, piloted by Tenente Pandolfo, shooting it down five miles south of Otocac, in Croatia. This kill was shared between Flt Lt Clifford Scott Vos in Mustang FB328/AK-V and South African 2Lt S W Pienaar. Of the downed Italian crew only Tenente Pandolfo took to his parachute and survived, although seriously wounded.

On 1 August P-47s strafed Villafranca, finishing off the damaged S.79-III B2-04. The defending flak claimed one Thunderbolt shot down.

August saw just one success and some losses for the *Aerosiluranti* of *Gruppo* 'Buscaglia', based in Greece. On the 4th three *Sparvieri* flown by Tenenti Luigi Morselli, Adriano Merani and Domenico De Lieto Vollaro torpedoed and damaged the 7100-ton British freighter *Samsylarna* north of Benghazi, the vessel duly being run aground on the Libyan coast with its engine room flooded. However, the following day two S.79-IIIs were lost. One ditched off Argos after running out of fuel and the other, flown by Maresciallo Jasinski, crashed into the sea off Crete with the loss of its entire crew.

These disheartening events led to the torpedo-bombers' repatriation. Six headed for Belgrade-Semlin, where five of them made a two-day stopover. The sixth refuelled at Pancevo airfield and headed for Italy on its own. On 11 August, while five 1° *Gruppo Sparvieri* were taking off for Lonate from Belgrade-Semlin, a disastrous mistake by German flak units caused another tragedy. Batteries fired at the five trimotors and shot down Tenente Morselli's aircraft, which crashed near the airport, killing all on board except the pilot. The remaining four aircraft scattered and returned separately to Italy, where the *gruppo* was deactivated for at least two months.

Tenente Francesco Pandolfo (left), with his co-pilot, Maresciallo Sesto Moschi. Both men received the Silver Medal for Military Valour and the Iron Cross 2nd Class for the June 1944 Gibraltar raid. On 31 July 1944 their S.79, B1-00, was intercepted by Mustang IIIs of No 213 Sqn and shot down south of Otocac, in Croatia. Only Tenente Pandolfo survived, taking to his parachute after being hurled out when the *Sparviero* exploded (*Nino Arena*)

During this period, on 25 August, the *gruppo*'s personnel faced Operation *Phoenix* – a German attempt to disband the ANR and set up an 'Italian Air Legion' under Luftwaffe control. At Lonate Pozzolo only seven (other sources say four) of the *gruppo*'s 854 airmen agreed to join the Germans, and the scheme failed.

After this lull in operations it was decided that 1° *Gruppo Aerosiluranti* should commence combat once again. On 12 October Maggiore Marini summoned his men, telling them that the *gruppo* was to change its designation. Knowing of Maggiore Buscaglia's tragic death while he was serving with the ICAF, Marini decreed that the unit would now be named in honour of Capitano Carlo Faggioni. The trimotors of the newly titled *Gruppo* 'Faggioni' therefore changed the prefix of their fuselage code letters from 'B' to 'F'.

Reorganisation started once again, and although several *Sparvieri* were strafed on 28 October 14 remained airworthy. Operations were set to resume in early November, but due to disagreements with the Germans and the usual setbacks, the unit remained grounded into December. As if this was not enough, on 26 December four P-47s strafed Lonate Pozzolo, destroying 12 *Sparvieri* on the ground (other sources state 14). The previous day, four S.79s had indeed taken off at 2130 hrs to attack shipping reported in Ancona harbour. Capitano Bertuzzi, in F1-01, claimed a 7000-ton ship hit (not confirmed by the Allies). Of the other three *Sparvieri*, F1-03 (Tenente Del Prete), F1-04 (Tenente Perina) and F1-06 (Tenente Neri), the second and third disengaged without dropping their torpedoes – Perina reported a failure of the release mechanism. All S.79s made it back to base without significant damage.

Obviously, the blow received on Boxing Day severely affected *Gruppo* 'Faggioni's' effectiveness. To recover from this disaster, it was planned to re-equip the unit with either Fw 190 or Fiat G.55 fighters, but this scheme never materialised.

On the evening of 5 January 1945 two S.79bis torpedo-bombers flown by Capitano Mannelli and Tenente Del Prete took off on what would prove to be *Gruppo* 'Faggioni's' last action, claiming a 5000-ton freighter sunk in the Adriatic. Unfortunately, this alleged success was again unconfirmed by Allied reports.

As if the unit had not endured enough trouble, on 13 January partisans captured Maggiore Marini near Novara while he was on his way to Turin. The officer 'enjoyed their hospitality' for about two months. During this period the *gruppo*'s activities were frequently hampered by partisan attacks. Near Gallarate on 14 March they ambushed three pilot officers, Sottotenenti Michele Cosimo Gulli, Italo Savi and Pietro Leonardi, killing them with sub-machine gun fire.

The *Gruppo* 'Faggioni's' men tried to equip their unit with G.55 fighters until 26-27 April, when they surrendered to partisans, thus officially ending their part in the war.

Altogether, through 1944-45 1° *Gruppo Aerosiluranti* had succeeded in damaging just one freighter (confirmed by the Allies) for the loss of about 100 airmen, comprising officer and under-officer pilots and other-ranks specialists. Eleven actions had been fought, during which 50 torpedoes were dropped.

To gauge the effectiveness of the S.79 as a torpedo-bomber, it is necessary to assess the *Aerosiluranti*'s performance over the entire conflict. The aircraft undoubtedly proved itself to be the most effective anti-shipping weapon Italy could field in the Mediterranean War. Although *Sparvieri* crews did not achieve outstanding successes against capital ships, they nevertheless managed to keep the Allies constantly on the alert with their bold and almost suicidal attacks.

During more than 37 months of war, from 15 August 1940 to 8 September 1943, the *Aerosiluranti* flew 2408 missions and lost 110 aircraft, although many aircrews were saved. Sardinia's *Aerosiluranti* flew 955 missions and lost 55 aircraft, while the Aegean units flew 593 missions for the loss of 20 aircraft. Next came the Sicilian units with 434 missions and 19 aircraft lost. The North African units reported 274 missions for the loss of six aircraft, while the south Italian units flew 152 missions and lost ten aircraft.

From 1940 to 1944 the *Regia Aeronautica* and ANR torpedo-bombers struck home 40 times (two torpedoes failed to explode), sinking 21 ships and damaging 17 others. These comprised nine warships (including three auxiliary units) and 12 freighters. In addition, 11 warships and six merchantmen were damaged. Comparing these results with those achieved by German torpedo-bombers, the Italians scored more warship successes (nine sunk and 11 damaged) than the Germans (three sunk and four damaged). As regards heavy-tonnage warships, the Italians damaged one battleship (using S.84s), one carrier and six cruisers, while the Germans could boast only the cruiser HMS *Arethusa* damaged. However, the Germans sank more merchant ships – a total of 31.

No one can deny that Italy's torpedo-bomber crews well deserved the laurels of fame they earned both during and after the war, not only in Italy but also abroad.

An ANR S.79 is armed with a torpedo prior to flying a mission during the winter of 1944. According to some source this aircraft was assigned to the *Squadriglia Addestramento* for crew training

APPENDICES

APPENDIX A

S.79 TORPEDO-BOMBER UNITS 1940-45

Reparto Sperimentale Aerosiluranti

Formed at Gorizia on 25 July 1940. Renamed *Reparto Speciale Aerosiluranti* (RSA) shortly thereafter. On 12 August 1940 moved to Berka (Benghazi), then to El Adem to begin operations. Attacked Alexandria harbour on 15 August 1940. On 3 September 1940 re-designated 278ª *Squadriglia Aut AS.*

278ª *Squadriglia Aut AS*

Formed on 3 September 1940 from RSA. In Cyrenaica, Libya, by December 1940 and Ain Gazala and Castel Benito, Libya, in January 1941. One section to Pantelleria on 15 February. *Squadriglia* HQ and one section to Gerbini, Sicily, on 14 May 1941, while rest of unit based at Pantelleria. Whole unit based at Castelvetrano, Sicily, in March 1942. By 1 April 1942 posted to newly constituted 132° *Gruppo.*

279ª *Squadriglia Aut AS*

Formed on 26 December 1940. From Gorizia, northeast Italy, moved to Catania-Fontanarossa, Sicily, on 28th of same month. January 1941 at Gerbini, then to Gadurra, Rhodes, on 14 April same year. There, took part in forming 34° *Gruppo AS* (which was disbanded in early July 1941). On 8 May 1941 moved to Cyrenaica, deploying three aircraft to Benghazi K2 and another three to Benina. 27 May shifted to El Fteiah, then to Benghazi K3 and to Misurata (15 and 19/21 December 1941, respectively). On 25 March 1942 became part of 131° *Gruppo Aut AS* formation.

280ª *Squadriglia Aut AS*

Formed at Gorizia on 8 February 1941. Unit moved to Elmas, Sardinia, on the 10th. There, in September 1941, unit took part in formation of 130° *Gruppo Autonomo*. Short Libyan tour (Castel Benito and Misurata) from 23 November to 28 December 1941.

281ª *Squadriglia Aut AS*

Formed at Grottaglie, Apulia, on 5 March 1941. Moved to Gadurra on 20th of same month. There, joined 34° *Gruppo* (disbanded by early July 1941). *Squadriglia* autonomous again on 1 July. Operations both from Rhodes and North Africa. Unit disbanded 1 January 1942, its aircraft and some crews posted to 41° *Gruppo AS*. *Squadriglia* re-established 1 April 1942 to serve with 278ª **Squadriglia** within new 132° *Gruppo Aut AS.*

283ª *Squadriglia Aut AS*

Formed at Rome-Ciampino on 4 July 1941 and moved to Elmas 11 days later. On 1 September 1941 took part in formation of 130° *Gruppo Aut AS*. Short Libyan tour (Castel Benito and Misurata) 23 November to 28 December 1941.

284ª *Squadriglia Aut AS*

Formed at Ciampino on 7 November 1941 and moved to Catania-Fontanarossa on 23 November. Four days later at Derna, Libya, then Benghazi K3 (15/16 December 1941) and to Misurata (20 December). On 13 February 1942 deployed at Benghazi K2. On 25 March 1942 unit and 279ª *Squadriglia* formed 131° *Gruppo Aut AS.*

34° *Gruppo Aut AS*

During November 1940 five S.79 torpedo-bombers and crews were posted to Gadurra. There, they joined 34° *Gruppo BT*, being divided between *gruppo*'s two sub-units, 67ª and 68ª *Squadriglie*. On 21 April 1941 *gruppo* converted to torpedo-bomber role (67ª and 68ª *Squadriglie* disbanded and replaced by 279ª and 281ª *Squadriglie*). On 8 May 1941 279ª *Squadriglia* moved to Cyrenaica. 34° *Gruppo* disbanded between 30 June and 3 July 1941. Thus, 281ª *Squadriglia* became autonomous on 1 July, receiving orders from *Aeronautica Egeo* Command.

41° *Gruppo Aut AS*

Former bomber unit (with 204ª and 205ª *Squadriglie*). On January 1941 moved to Littoria, central Italy, partly converting to torpedo-bomber role and re-equipping with S.84s. After elementary training, unit posted back to Aegean with a mixed force of S.79s and S.84s. Due to S.84's poor performance, in January 1942 41° *Gruppo* received S.79s and personnel from disbanded 281ª and 282ª *Squadriglie AS*. On February 1942 last S.84s disposed of and unit repatriated on 2 August, moving to Pisa-San Giusto. In November 1942 *gruppo* received brand-new S.79s built by Reggiane. In April 1943 205ª *Squadriglia* based at Decimomannu, Sardinia. On 25 May 204ª *Squadriglia* moved to Siena-Ampugnano. There, some days later, the sub-unit joined *Rgpt AS*. At beginning of July 1943 205ª *Squadriglia* also joined 204ª *Squadriglia* at Siena-Ampugnano. There, kept an alarm section that, in turns of ten days each, returned to Sardinia, performing alarm duties. Through July to August 1943 204ª *Squadriglia* based at Gioia del Colle, Apulia. *Gruppo* disbanded on 1 February 1944.

130° *Gruppo Aut AS*

Formed at Elmas on 1 September 1941 with 281ª and 283ª *Squadriglie* (formerly autonomous units). *Gruppo* operated mainly from Sardinia up to February 1943. To Catania mid-November 1941. Short Libyan tour, 23 November to 28 December 1941. To May 1942 aircraft from both *squadriglie* were detached to Pantelleria. Moved to Villacidro in November 1942. In March 1943 re-organised at Littoria. Lack of equipment led to *gruppo* disbandment in summer of 1943, crews posted to *Rgpt AS.*

131° *Gruppo Aut AS*

Formed at Benghazi K2 on 25 March 1942 with formerly autonomous 279ª and 284ª *Squadriglie*. From June 1942 unit operated from El Fteiah, Derna and Mersa Matruh airfields, then repatriating in November. In April 1943 279ª *Squadriglia* was at Gerbini, replacing 132° *Gruppo,* which was moving to Gorizia. 284ª *Squadriglia* remained at Pisa-San Giusto, where in June 1943 joined *Rgpt AS.*

132° *Gruppo Aut AS*

This famous unit formed at Littoria on 1 April 1942 with 281ª *Squadriglia* and Castelvetrano-based 278ª *Squadriglia*. HQ to Gerbini 2 May 1942 (281ª *Squadriglia* there since late April). Whole unit at Castelvetrano on 14 June 1942. To Pantelleria 11 August. Mid-November 1942 unit back to Castelvetrano. To Trapani-Chinisia 10 December. January 1943 temporary deployment to

Decimomannu. March 1943 unit returned to Gerbini, then moved to Gorizia in April. Summer 1943 saw unit reorganised at Littoria, operating mainly from this base. *Gruppo* scored its last success the day before armistice.

133° *Gruppo Aut AS*

Formed at Benghazi K2 early April 1942 with 174ª and 175ª *Squadriglie* (former reconnaissance units). July 1942 saw *Gruppo* HQ and 174ª *Squadriglia* based at Benghazi K3, 175ª *Squadriglia* being detached at Castel Benito. After converting to torpedo-bomber role, *gruppo* actually flew naval escort and attack reconnaissance duties. Repatriated on 24 November 1942, *gruppo* moved to Pisa-San Giusto. Earlier that month some crews and aircraft had been transferred to Misurata-based 21ª *Squadriglia*, other crews being posted to 131° *Gruppo*. *Gruppo* was officially disbanded at the end of December 1942.

32° *Stormo AS*

Another former S.79 bomber unit, converted to torpedo-bomber role on 1 May 1942. Of its two sub-units only 89° *Gruppo* performed the role, however, 38° *Gruppo* continuing bomber operations. The unit, S.84-equipped, was at Gioia del Colle, Apulia, by 28 May 1942. Through August 1942 89° *Gruppo* was first deployed at Villacidro, Sardinia, then its 229ª *Squadriglia* alone returned to Gioia del Colle. 228ª *Squadriglia* moved to Naples-Capodichino on 16 August 1942. During November/December 1942 whole unit deployed in Sardinia at Milis and Alghero. On 21 December 1942 89° *Gruppo* returned to Gioia del Colle then exchanged its S.84s (to 38° *Gruppo*) for S.79s (from 108° *Gruppo*), becoming autonomous. First half of 1943 89° *Gruppo* based in Sardinia. In early January 1943 *Stormo* temporarily reconverted to bomber role, moving to Lecce along with 38° *Gruppo*. On 27 January 1943 the *Stormo* was deactivated. On June 1943 89° *Gruppo* joined *Rgpt AS* at Siena-Ampugnano, but as of 8 August 1943 *gruppo* was disbanded.

36° *Stormo AS*

After operations as bomber unit from Sicily, on November 1940 this *Stormo* returned to Bologna, there transitioning to S.84s. After training, the unit converted to torpedo-bomber role on 1 September 1941, two days later moving to Decimomannu with its 108° *Gruppo*. This *gruppo* was joined by its twin sub-unit, 109° *Gruppo*, on 20 September 1941. *Stormo* remained in Sardinia until 12 September 1942, next day handing over some of its S.84s to 32° *Stormo* at Gioia del Colle. In early November 1942 unit was back at Decimomannu, but around mid-December 1942 handed over its S.79s to 89° *Gruppo*. Then all *stormo* returned to Pisa. There, its crews underwent night torpedo training. By 22 May 1943 *stormo* again flew frontline operations, mainly from Milis and Gerbini. In June 1943 108° *Gruppo* joined with *Rgpt AS,* becoming autonomous as of 15 July 1943 after 36° *Stormo* and 109° *Gruppo* disbandment. *Stormo* awarded *Medaglia d'Oro al Valor Militare*.

46° *Stormo AS*

Former bomber unit converted to torpedo-bomber role on in February 1942. On 13 June part of its 104° *Gruppo* took off from Decimomannu to attack *Harpoon* convoy, and on 30 June moved to Gadurra. From 11 to 15 August its twin 105° *Gruppo* was in turn at Decimomannu, then Pisa. *Stormo* was disbanded on 1 September 1942, its two *gruppi* becoming autonomous. 104° *Gruppo* operated from Gadurra up to 12 July 1943, when repatriated. 253ª *Squadriglia* to Crete (Heraklion) 22 June to 12 July 1943. Through July 104° *Gruppo* was based firstly at Lecce, then at Rimini and later at Siena-Ampungano. After operations in Sicily, armistice surprised 104° *Gruppo* while it was still in action against Allied shipping off Salerno. After temporary deployment to Sardinia, all 104° *Gruppo* crews and aircraft merged into 253ª *Squadriglia*. This sub-unit joined 132° *Gruppo*, returning to Lecce after deployments to US bases at Catania and Korba, Tunisia. From 12 September 1942 105° *Gruppo* was based again at Decimomannu, then moved to Forlì in May 1943. Disbanded by 6 June 1943. *Stormo* awarded *Medaglia d'Oro al Valor Militare*.

Reparto Speciale Aerosiluranti

Long-range S.79bis unit, also entitled *Gruppo Speciale*. Formed February 1943 for Operation *Scoglio* (attack on Gibraltar 19/20 June 1943). Based at Istres, southern France. Another North African mission flown on 24/25 June. Repatriated June 1943 and then disbanded.

Raggruppamento Siluranti

Formed on 1 June 1943 with 284ª *Squadriglia* and 108° *Gruppo* at Pisa-San Giusto and 204ª *Squadriglia* with 89° *Gruppo* at Siena-Ampugnano. Sicilian ops from Apulia. Disbanded on September 1943 after armistice.

1° *Gruppo* ANR 'Buscaglia'/'Faggioni'

Officially formed on 1 January 1944 at Venegono. Made up of 1ª, 2ª and 3ª *Squadriglie* plus one training *Squadriglia Complementare*. Based at Venegono, Lonate Pozzolo, Perugia Sant'Egidio (ALG), Gorizia and Castano Primo. Night operations off Anzio in spring 1944. *Squadriglia Complementare* disbanded 31 May 1944, replaced by *Squadriglia Addestramento AS* and *Squadriglia Scuola AS*. July-August 1944 at Eleusis, Greece, for eastern Mediterranean ops. Renamed 'Faggioni' Group on 12 October 1944. Disbanded 27 April 1945.

1° *Nucleo Addestramento Aerosiluranti*

Formed at Gorizia on 26 October 1940. To Capodichino 1 to 15 April 1941, then back to Gorizia. After armistice crews and aircraft formed AR torpedo unit.

2° *Nucleo Addestramento Aerosiluranti*

Formed at Naples-Capodichino on 25 November 1940. August 1942 attacks on *Pedestal* convoy. Disbanded September 1943 owing to lack of aircraft.

3° *Nucleo Addestramento Aerosiluranti*

Formed at Pisa-San Giusto on 15 January 1942. On 13 June 1942 it provided three crews to attack *Harpoon* convoy. 11 to 13 August 1942 some crews attacked *Pedestal* convoy. Operation *Torch* attacks. 1 July 1943 moved to Salon-en-Provence, France. September 1943 all crews and aircraft captured by Germans.

APPENDIX B

S.79 WARSHIP KILLS 1940-43

DATE	SHIP	TYPE	LOCATION	S.79 UNIT	RESULTS
17/9/40	HMS *Kent*	cruiser	northeast of Bardia	278ª *Squadriglia*	damaged (Robone and Buscaglia)
14/10/40	HMS *Liverpool*	cruiser	south of Crete	278ª *Squadriglia*	damaged (Erasi)
3/12/40	HMS *Glasgow*	cruiser	Souda Bay	278ª *Squadriglia*	damaged (Erasi and Buscaglia)
23/7/41	HMS *Fearless*	destroyer	La Galite	283ª *Squadriglia*	sunk (Pandolfi)
23/7/41	HMS *Manchester*	cruiser	La Galite	283ª *Squadriglia*	damaged (Di Bella)
11/8/41	HMS *Protector*	netlayer	northwest of Port Said	281ª *Squadriglia*	damaged (Buscaglia)
27/8/41	HMS *Phoebe*	cruiser	north of Bardia	279ª *Squadriglia*	damaged (Marini)
23/11/41	HMS *Glenroy*	landing ship infantry	north of Mersa Matruh	281ª *Squadriglia*	damaged (Buscaglia and Rovelli)
1/12/41	HMS *Jackal*	destroyer	Mersa Luch	279ª *Squadriglia*	damaged
5/12/41	HMS *Chakdina*	armed boarding ship	Mersa Luch	279ª *Squadriglia*	sunk (Ranieri)
14/6/42	HMS *Liverpool*	cruiser	south of Sardinia	104°/130° *Gruppi*	damaged
15/6/42	HMS *Bedouin*	destroyer	southwest of Pantelleria	132° *Gruppo*	sunk (Aichner)
22/7/42	HMS *Malines*	auxiliary escort ship	off Port Said	205ª *Squadriglia*	fatally disabled (Cionni and Coloni)
12/8/42	HMS *Foresight*	destroyer	northwest of Cani Island	132° *Gruppo*	sunk
10/11/42	HMS *Ibis*	sloop	north of Algiers	130° *Gruppo*	sunk
9/12/42	HMS *Marigold*	corvette	Algiers Bay	105° *Gruppo*	sunk
29/1/43	HMS *Pozarica*	AA auxiliary ship	Bougie	105°/130°/132° *Gruppi*	later sunk
16/7/43	HMS *Indomitable*	carrier	south of Cape Passero	*Rgpt AS*	damaged (Capelli)
15/8/43	LST-414	landing ship, tank	Cani Island	132° *Gruppo*	sunk (Faggioni)
7/9/43	LST-417	landing ship, tank	off Termini	132° *Gruppo*	beached (Pagliarusco)

APPENDIX C

S.79 MERCHANT SHIP KILLS 1941-44

DATE	SHIP	TYPE/COUNTRY	LOCATION	S.79 UNIT	RESULTS
18/4/41	*British Science*	tanker /UK	Kasos Strait	279ª *Squadriglia*	damaged (Barbani and Caponetti)
18/4/41	*British Science*	tanker /UK	Kasos Strait	281ª *Squadriglia*	sunk (Cimicci)
8/5/41	*Rawnsley*	motorship/UK	south of Crete	281ª *Squadriglia*	beached, later sunk by Germans
24/7/41	*Hoegh Hood*	tanker/Norway	La Galite	280ª *Squadriglia*	damaged (Mojoli and Rivoli)
20/8/41	*Turbo*	tanker/UK	north of Port Said	281ª *Squadriglia*	fatally disabled (Forzinetti)
27/8/41	*Deucalion*	steamer/UK	south of Sardinia	280ª *Squadriglia*	hit/unexploded torpedo (Setti)
27/9/41	*Imperial Star*	steamer/UK	Skerki	278ª *Squadriglia*	sunk (Magagnoli)
24/10/41	*Empire Guillemot*	steamer/UK	La Galite	130° *Gruppo*	sunk (Focacci)
14/11/41	*Empire Pelican*	steamer/UK	La Galite	130° *Gruppo*	sunk (Barioglio)
9/6/42	*Stureborg*	steamer/Sweden	south of Cyprus	204/205ª *Squadriglie*	sunk (Vicarotti and Pucci)
14/6/42	*Tanimbar*	steamer/the Netherlands	south of Sardinia	104° *Gruppo*	shared sunk with 9° *Stormo*
30/6/42	*Aircrest*	steamer/UK	west of Jaffa	205ª *Squadriglia*	sunk (Pucci)
13/8/42	*Port Chalmers*	steamer/UK	west of Malta	132° *Gruppo*	hit/unexploded torpedo
23/11/42	*Scythia*	steamer/UK	off Algiers	283ª *Squadriglia*	damaged/KG 26 attack also
28/11/42	*Selbo*	steamer/Norway	north of Cape Cavallo	108°/132° *Gruppi*	sunk
6/2/43	*Al Ameriaah*	motor sailing ship/Egypt	north of Alexandria	104° *Gruppo*	sunk
27/3/43	*Empire Rowan*	motorship/UK	Philippeville Gulf	105° *Gruppo*	sunk (Mancini KIA)
16/8/43	*Benjamin Contee*	steamer/USA	off Bone	132° *Gruppi*	damaged (Terzi)
16/8/43	*Empire Kestrel*	steamer/UK	off Cape Bougaroun	132° *Gruppo*	sunk (Cimicchi)
4/8/44	*Samsylarna*	steamer/UK	north of Benghazi	1° *Gruppo* ANR	damaged

APPENDIX D

S.79 GOLD MEDAL FOR MILITARY VALOUR RECIPIENTS

RANK AND NAME	UNIT	REMARKS
Maresciallo di 3ª classe Vito Sinisi	279ª *Squadriglia Aut AS*	Died of wounds 24/6/41
Sergente Maggiore Riccardo Balagna	279ª *Squadriglia Aut AS*	Died of wounds 24/6/41
Tenente Pietro Donà delle Rose	283ª *Squadriglia Aut AS*	Killed in action 27/8/41
Tenente Giulio Cesare Graziani	281ª *Squadriglia Aut AS*, 132° *Gruppo AS* and RSA	Died 23/12/98
Tenente Aldo Forzinetti	281ª *Squadriglia Aut AS*	Killed in action 17/12/41
Tenente Luigi Rovelli	281ª *Squadriglia Aut AS*	Killed in action 28/12/41
Tenente Franco Cappa	280ª *Squadriglia Aut AS*	Killed in action 8/5/41
Tenente di Vascello Antonio Forni	283ª *Squadriglia Aut AS*	Died of exposure 27/8/41
Tenente Mario Ingrellini	253ª *Squadriglia*, 104° *Gruppo AS*	Killed in action 14/6/42
Sergente Maggiore Giorgio Compiani	253ª *Squadriglia*, 104° *Gruppo AS*	Killed in action 14/6/42
Tenente Lelio Silva	2° *Nucleo AS*	Killed in action 15/6/42
Sottotenente Martino Aichner	132° *Gruppo AS*	Died 21/12/94
Tenente Silvio Angelucci	105° *Gruppo AS*	Killed in action 13/8/42
Aviere Scelto Francesco Maiore	132° *Gruppo AS*	Died of wounds 27/11/42
Maggiore Carlo Emanuele Buscaglia	RSA, 278ª and 281ª *Squadriglie* and 132° *Gruppo AS*	Died of wounds 24/8/44
Sottotenente Antonio Vellere	130° *Gruppo AS*	Killed in action 2/12/42
Sottotenente Carlo Pfister	132° *Gruppo AS*	Killed in flying accident 28/2/43
Capitano Urbano Mancini	105° *Gruppo AS*	Killed in action 27/3/43
Capitano Francesco Aurelio Di Bella	283ª *Squadriglia*, 3° *Nucleo AS* and RSA	Died 4/72
Capitano Giuseppe Cimicchi	281ª *Squadriglia*, 130° and 132° *Gruppi AS* and RSA	Died 15/10/92
Tenente Colonnello Vittorio Cannaviello	34° *Gruppo*, 2° *Nucleo AS* and 132° *Gruppo AS*	Missing in action 12/8/43
Maggiore Massimiliano Erasi	278ª and 284ª *Squadriglie*, 1° *Nucleo AS* and 130° and 41° *Gruppi*	Killed in action 21/2/45
Tenente di Vascello (later Capitano di Corvetta) Oss Domenico Baffigo	279ª *Squadriglia Aut AS*	Killed in action by Germans 11/9/43
Capitano Carlo Faggioni	281ª and 278ª *Squadriglie*, 132° *Gruppo* RSA (RA) and 1° *Gruppo* (AR)	RSI award Killed in action 10/4/44

COLOUR PLATES

1
S.79 '6' of Maggiore Vincenzo Dequal, CO of *Reparto Speciale Aerosiluranti*, El Adem, Libya, August 1940

As with the other aircraft of this unit, S.79 '6' features the typical standard camouflage worn by Italian aircraft in the early stages of the war – uppersurfaces painted in *verde* and *marrone mimetico* (camouflage green and brown) mottling over a *giallo mimetico* (camouflage yellow) background, with *alluminio* (aluminium/silver) undersides. This aircraft took part in the operational debut of Italian *Aerosiluranti*, attacking Alexandria harbour on 15 August 1940. Then, after the RSA was re-designated 278ª *Squadriglia*, this aircraft, recoded 278-6 and flown by the unit's new CO, Capitano Massimiliano Erasi, torpedoed and badly damaged the British cruisers HMS *Liverpool* and HMS *Glasgow* on 14 October and 3 December 1940, respectively.

2
S.79 278-2 of Tenente Carlo Emanuele Buscaglia, 278ª *Squadriglia Autonoma Aerosiluranti*, El Adem, Libya, September 1940

Flying this aircraft, rising torpedo ace Buscaglia participated in the actions in which the light cruisers HMS *Kent* and HMS *Glasgow* were torpedoed, on 17 September and 3 December 1940, respectively. In the latter action Buscaglia personally scored a hit on HMS *Glasgow*.

3
S.79 278-1 of Tenente Guido Robone, 278ª *Squadriglia Autonoma Aerosiluranti*, El Adem, Libya, late summer 1940

An interesting feature of Robone's aircraft was the application of black Xs beneath the wings, inboard of the national insignia roundels. These were applied to Italian aircraft operating in North Africa in order to avoid further (potentially lethal) identification mistakes after Marshal Italo Balbo's S.79 was shot down by anti-aircraft fire from Italian guns defending Tobruk on 28 June 1940. Piloting this aircraft, Tenente Robone scored (along with Tenente Buscaglia) 278ª *Squadriglia*'s first confirmed kill, successfully torpedoing the cruiser HMS *Kent* on 17 September 1940.

4

S.79 278-3 of 278ª *Squadriglia Autonoma Aerosiluranti*, Sicily, spring 1941

According to some sources this S.79 has been identified as MM23881, which, piloted by Capitano Oscar Cimolini, was posted as missing in action on 21 April 1941. Its wreck, with the remains of some of its crew, was discovered between 21 July and 5 October 1960 in the Libyan desert, about 400 km (250 miles) south of Benghazi. This doomed S.79 has its uppersurfaces painted with a *giallo mimetico* (camouflage yellow) mottling over a *verde mimetico* (camouflage green) background. Its undersurfaces are painted in *grigio mimetico* (camouflage grey) and the propeller spinners are light blue-grey. Photographic evidence has enabled researchers to identify this S.79's codes as 278-3. A little clear mottling over numeral '8' of the unit code appears in three different photos at least, thus adding further clues to its identification. Worth noting on the fuselage is a yellow-edged roundel encircling the legendary *'Quattro Gatti'* (four cats) unit emblem.

5

S.79 281-5 of Capitano Carlo Emanuele Buscaglia, CO of 281ª *Squadriglia Autonoma Aerosiluranti*, Gadurra, Rhodes, summer 1941

This aircraft was Buscaglia's usual mount in many torpedo actions flown over the eastern Mediterranean through 1941. 281ª *Squadriglia*'s war diary records two aircraft usually flown by Buscaglia in action, MM23877 and MM23838. This trimotor is finished with a mixed scheme of *verde mimetico* and *marrone mimetico* (camouflage green and brown) mottles over a *giallo mimetico* (camouflage yellow) background. The undersurfaces are in *grigio mimetico* (camouflage grey), although another source reports the undersides as being in aluminium. The spinners are *grigio azzurro chiaro* (light blue-grey). In order to reduce its visibility the aircraft's frontal areas were also painted in *grigio azzurro chiaro*.

6

S.79 '9' of 1° *Nucleo Addestramento Aerosiluranti*, Gorizia, northern Italy, late 1941

The *Nuclei AS* was tasked with the training of torpedo aircrews, often providing its own crews and aircraft for operational actions. The CO of 1° *Nucleo AS* was the remarkable Tenente Colonnello Carlo Unia, a prominent officer of the *Aerosiluranti*. This S.79 features a mixed mottling of *verde mimetico* (camouflage green) and *marrone mimetico* (camouflage brown) over a *giallo mimetico* (camouflage yellow) background, with *grigio azzurro chiaro* (light blue-grey) undersides. Markings comprise a black-painted individual numeral '9' inside the white fuselage band. The aircraft sports the plain white tail cross without the Savoy crest. White identification bands typical of torpedo-bombers being used for training are painted outboard of the wing roundels, both on the uppersurfaces and on the undersides. There are black national roundels on a clear background on the upperwing surfaces, while the underwing roundels are black-trimmed and have three black fasces on a white background. Fuselage fasces inside a white-bordered blue roundel are on the central engine cowling.

7

S.79 278-1 of 278ª *Squadriglia Autonoma Aerosiluranti*, Gerbini, Sicily, May 1941

On 14 May 1941 the 278ª *Squadriglia* staff moved to Gerbini, in Sicily, the unit being led in succession through that year by Capitani Massimiliano Erasi, Dante Magagnoli and Ugo Rivoli. On 27 September 1941 Magagnoli sank the large transport *Imperial Star* during Operation *Halberd*. This S.79 displays an interesting camouflage scheme, with uppersurfaces in *giallo*

mimetico (camouflage yellow) mottles over a *verde mimetico* (camouflage green) background. The undersides are *grigio mimetico* (camouflage grey). The markings comprise a plain white tail cross lacking the Savoy crest, a black unit code and a red individual numeral, partly superimposed on the white fuselage band. There are fuselage fasces inside a blue roundel on the engine cowling and the spinners are grey. The overwing roundels are black on a clear background, while those below the wings are black-edged, having black fasces on a white background. The engine cowlings are yellow. In Italian aviation units (with some exceptions) the individual numeral '1' usually identified the aircraft flown by the CO.

8

S.79 279-3 of 279ª *Squadriglia Autonoma Aerosiluranti*, Mediterranean, spring 1941

This aircraft of 279ª *Squadriglia*, which, in 1941, led by Capitano Giulio Marini, saw many successful actions against British warships in the Mediterranean, features an experimental mixed camouflage on the fuselage and engine cowlings of large mottles in *verde mimetico* (camouflage green) and *marrone mimetico* (camouflage brown) over a *giallo mimetico* (camouflage yellow) background. The forward cockpit area and undersides are painted in *grigio azzurro chiaro* (light blue-grey).

9

S.79 283-8 of 283ª *Squadriglia Autonoma Aerosiluranti*, Elmas, Sardinia, August 1941

27 August 1941 was a busy day for 283ª *Squadriglia*. Firstly, two of the unit's S.79s (flown by Capitano Grossi and Tenente Barioglio) took off at 1135 hrs and intercepted a French cruiser entering Philippeville harbour. Both aircraft returned at 1500 hrs. In the afternoon Tenente Donà delle Rose heroically lost his life while attacking the steamer *Deucalion*. The unit's S.79 283-8 has a white tail cross complete with the Savoy crest in its centre, and unit and individual codes painted in light blue-grey aft of the white fuselage band. The roundels are black on a clear background both above and below the wings. The engine cowlings are yellow. As for camouflage, the uppersurfaces feature large mottles of *verde mimetico* (camouflage green) and little mottles of *marrone mimetico* (camouflage brown) over a *giallo mimetico* (camouflage yellow) background. The undersides are *grigio mimetico* (camouflage grey). The spinners are white.

10

S.79 283-5 of 283ª *Squadriglia*, 130° *Gruppo Autonomo Aerosiluranti*, Elmas, Sardinia, winter 1942

Some black-and-white photographs show 130° *Gruppo* aircraft in uniform camouflage, either *grigio azzurro scuro* (dark blue-grey, often very faded owing to salt and sun weathering) or *grigio azzurro chiaro* (light blue-grey, similar to faded dark blue-grey) overall. Dark olive green (also faded) and light green overall were possible camouflage alternatives. These schemes were complemented by undersurfaces painted in *grigio azzurro chiaro* (light blue-grey). The 283ª *Squadriglia* war diary records that on 26 November 1942 S.79 MM21861/283-5, flown by Sottotenente Vellere, moved with four other *Sparvieri* from Villacidro to Elmas.

11

S.79 of 2° *Nucleo Addestramento Aerosiluranti*, Naples-Capodichino, winter 1942

This aircraft sports a classical *Regia Aeronautica* camouflage scheme, featuring mixed mottling of *verde mimetico* (camouflage green) and *marrone mimetico* (camouflage brown) over a *giallo mimetico* (camouflage yellow) background. The undersides are *grigio azzurro chiaro* (light blue-grey). Its markings are also interesting, showing a white Savoy tail cross with the Savoy crest in the centre, a white fuselage identification band and white engine cowlings to denote its training role. The spinners are also white. The wing roundels are in black over clear backgrounds, both above and below the wings.

12

S.79 279-5 of 279ª *Squadriglia*, 131° *Gruppo Autonomo Aerosiluranti*, Mediterranean, spring 1942

This *Sparviero* has engine cowling fasces inside a black-trimmed blue roundel. The wing roundels are black on a clear background above and below the wings. There is a light blue unit code and dash with a red individual numeral. There is an oversprayed white fuselage identification band and a white Savoy tail cross with the Savoy crest in the centre. The uppersurfaces are *verde oliva scuro* (dark olive green) overall, while the undersides and spinners are both *grigio azzurro chiaro* (light blue-grey).

13

S.79 278-11 of 278ª *Squadriglia*, 132° *Gruppo Autonomo Aerosiluranti*, Catania, Sicily, spring 1942

From 1 April 1942 278ª *Squadriglia* joined 281ª *Squadriglia* to form 132° *Gruppo Autonomo Aerosiluranti*, led by ace Capitano Buscaglia. It was destined to become a legendary torpedo-bomber unit. This trimotor has a light blue unit code and red individual numerals. The white fuselage band has been toned down by overspraying and the white tail cross has the Savoy crest in its centre. The fuselage fasces are inside a black-edged blue roundel on the engine cowling, and wing roundels are black on a clear background, both above and below the wings. The uppersurfaces and gondola are *verde oliva scuro* (dark olive green) overall, while the undersurfaces and spinners are *grigio azzurro chiaro* (light blue-grey).

14

S.79 MM21434 284-4 of 284ª *Squadriglia Autonoma Aerosiluranti*, Benghazi K2, Libya, January 1942

This *Sparviero* displays a finish made up of large patches of *verde mimetico chiaro* and *scuro* (camouflage light and dark green) over a *giallo mimetico* (camouflage yellow) background. The undersurfaces are *grigio azzurro chiaro* (light blue-grey) and the spinners are white. An autonomous unit at the beginning of 1942, 284ª *Squadriglia* was paired with 279ª *Squadriglia* when 131° *Gruppo Autonomo Aerosiluranti* was created on 25 March that year.

15

S.79 MM23973 280-6 of Capitano Franco Melley, CO of 130° *Gruppo Autonomo Aerosiluranti*, Sardinia, spring 1942

Capitano Franco Melley flew this aircraft on several sorties in 1942, attacking both the carrier HMS *Argus* and the cruiser HMS *Cairo*, along with their naval escorts. MM23973 had also been previously used by Maggiore Erasi when 130° *Gruppo* sank the sloop HMS *Ibis* on 10 November 1942. Melley's usual mount features a *Gruppo* CO's red-striped blue command pennant on its fuselage beneath the dorsal machine gun position. The uppersurfaces and spinners are *grigio azzurro scuro* (dark blue-grey), partly faded and worn by the effects of sun and seawater. Faded green was a possible alternative. The undersides are *grigio azzurro chiaro* (light blue-grey).

16

S.79 175-4 of 175ª *Squadriglia*, 133° *Gruppo Autonomo Aerosiluranti*, Libya, spring 1942

On 1 April 1942 the formerly autonomous *Ricognizione Strategica Terrestre* (land-based long-range reconnaissance) 174ª and 175ª *Squadriglie* were formed into 133° *Gruppo Autonomo Aerosiluranti*. This unit was rarely employed in its planned torpedo-bomber role, however, instead flying many naval escorts and dangerous ground-attack sorties. This aircraft has a white Savoy tail cross apparently (from photographic

evidence) lacking the Savoy crest. The fuselage displays a black unit code and red individual numeral superimposed on a white band. The wing roundels are black on a clear background above and below the wings. There are fuselage fasces inside a blue roundel on the engine cowling. The aircraft has an unusual camouflage scheme consisting of long irregular streaks in *verde* and *marrone mimetico* (camouflage green and brown) over a *giallo mimetico* (camouflage yellow) background.

17

S.79 204-5 of 204ª *Squadriglia*, 41° *Gruppo Autonomo Aerosiluranti*, Gadurra, Rhodes, summer 1942

Led by the highly decorated Tenente Colonnello Ettore Muti, 41° *Gruppo* was very active over the eastern Mediterranean throughout 1942. This *Sparviero* displays a white tail cross apparently lacking the Savoy crest (according to a photograph). The fuselage bears a white unit code and red individual numeral. The national roundels are black on a clear background above and below the wings. The fuselage fasces on the engine cowling are set inside a black-edged blue roundel. The uppersurfaces, gondola and spinners are finished in *verde oliva scuro* (dark olive green) overall, while the undersurfaces are *grigio azzurro chiaro* (light blue-grey). The torpedo nose cone was probably red.

18

S.79 205-5 of 205ª *Squadriglia*, 41° *Gruppo Autonomo Aerosiluranti*, Rhodes, summer 1942

On 22 July 1942 two 205ª *Squadriglia* S.79s flown by Sottotenenti Dorando Cionni and Ferruccio Coloni torpedoed and fatally disabled the British escort ship HMS *Malines* northeast of Port Said, Egypt. This 205ª *Squadriglia* machine sports a white tail cross lacking the Savoy crest. Its unit code is light blue and the individual numeral is red. The fuselage band has been overpainted in black and the spinners are white. The wings carry national roundels in black on a clear background on both upper and undersurfaces. Finally, it too has *verde oliva scuro* (dark olive green) uppersurfaces and *grigio azzurro chiaro* (light blue-grey) undersides.

19

S.79 205-6 of Sottotenente Emilio Pucci, 205ª *Squadriglia*, 41° *Gruppo Autonomo Aerosiluranti*, Rhodes, June 1942

Photographic evidences show that this S.79 was the usual mount of Sottotenente Pucci, who ranked among torpedo aces after he sank the Swedish steamer *Stureborg* and the British ship *Aircrest*, both in June 1942. A Florentine nobleman, Pucci survived the war and later became a world famous fashion designer. Worthy of note is the rhomboidal-shaped dash between the codes, half-painted in red and faded light blue. The fuselage fasces are inside a black-trimmed blue roundel on the engine cowling. The S.79's uppersurfaces are painted *verde oliva scuro* (dark olive green), as are its spinners and ventral gondola. The aircraft's undersides are *grigio azzurro chiaro* (light blue-grey).

20

S.79 253-8 of 253ª *Squadriglia*, 104° *Gruppo*, 46° *Stormo Aerosiluranti*, Mediterranean, mid-summer 1942

This 104° *Gruppo* aircraft has white ship 'kill' silhouettes on its fin, denoting the unit's claimed successes. Noteworthy among these profiles are a battleship and a carrier strongly resembling HMS *Argus*. The aircraft has a white tail cross with the Savoy crest in the centre, a black unit code and a red individual numeral. The wing roundels are black on a clear background above the wings, and black-trimmed with black fasces on a white background under the wings. The fuselage fasces are inside a black-edged blue roundel on the engine cowling. The overall finish is *verde mimetico* (camouflage green) and *marrone mimetico* (camouflage brown) mottling over a *giallo mimetico* (camouflage yellow) background. The undersides, spinners and forward areas are *grigio azzurro chiaro* (light blue-grey).

21
S.79 278-1 of 132° *Gruppo Autonomo Aerosiluranti,* Sicily, late 1942

This aircraft is clearly the mount of 132° *Gruppo*'s commanding officer. Through late 1942 the COs of this renowned unit were, in succession, Maggiore Buscaglia (shot down over Bougie on 12 November 1942), Capitano Graziani (temporary) and, finally, Maggiore Gabriele Casini. This interesting trimotor has a white tail cross with the Savoy crest on its upper vertical arm. The 132° *Gruppo* badge is on the fin, and other markings include a light blue unit code partly superimposed over the white fuselage band, plus a red individual numeral. The nickname *Sparviero* is inscribed ahead of the cockpit, and on the fuselage side beneath the dorsal gun position there is a red-striped blue command pennant. The usual fuselage fasces inside a blue roundel are on the engine cowling. The wing roundels are black on a clear background both above and below the wings. The uppersurfaces are painted in a uniform *verde oliva scuro* (dark olive green) finish, while the undersurfaces are painted in *grigio azzurro chiaro* (light blue-grey). The spinners are blue.

22
S.79 205-3 of 205ª *Squadriglia,* 41° *Gruppo Autonomo Aerosiluranti,* Pisa-San Giusto, Tuscany, winter 1942-43

After long service in the Aegean, 41° *Gruppo* was repatriated to Pisa-San Giusto in August 1942. This aircraft has a white tail cross with the Savoy crest in its centre, a black unit code and a red individual numeral. Its fuselage band has also been darkened. The wing roundels are black on a clear background above and below the wings, and the fuselage fasces are inside a blue roundel on the engine cowling. Its camouflage comprises *verde oliva scuro* (dark olive green) uppersurfaces, spinners and gondola and *grigio azzurro chiaro* (light blue-grey) undersides.

23
S.79 254-1 of 254ª *Squadriglia,* 105° *Gruppo Autonomo Aerosiluranti,* Sardinia, late 1942

105° *Gruppo* was heavily engaged opposing both the *Pedestal* (led by Tenente Colonnello Cadringher) and *Torch* (led by Capitano Urbano Mancini) operations. *Sparviero* 254-1 was flown by both Cadringher and Mancini, on 12 and 13 August 1942, respectively. It was then piloted in action by Tenente Michele Avalle on 11 November 1942, and by Capitano Mancini again on 9 December 1942, when a trio of 254ª *Squadriglia* aircraft sank HMS *Marigold*. On 27 March 1943 Mancini accounted for the freighter *Empire Rowan*, but this success cost him his life. This trimotor has a white tail cross with the Savoy crest in the centre, a black unit code and a red individual numeral. The roundels are black on a clear background above and below the wings. The fuselage fasces are inside a blue roundel on the engine cowling, and there is a standard *'Divieto di caccia'* ('hunting forbidden') unit badge on the fin. The S.79's unusual camouflage scheme consists of *grigio azzurro chiaro* (light blue-grey) thickly mottled over a *verde oliva scuro* (dark olive green) background. The cockpit hump, undersides and propeller hubs are also painted in light blue-grey.

24
S.79 253-10 of Tenente Alberto Dattrino, 253ª *Squadriglia,* 104° *Gruppo Autonomo Aerosiluranti,* Rhodes, April 1943

This aircraft was badly damaged after it swung on takeoff from Rhodes on 17 April 1943, the crew escaping the accident unharmed. It has the usual white tail cross with the Savoy crest at its centre, a black unit code and a red individual numeral. On the engine cowling are the fuselage fasces, inside a black-edged blue roundel, and the propeller hubs are black. The roundels are black on a clear background above and below the wings. The camouflage comprises sharp-edged *grigio azzurro chiaro* (light blue-grey) splotches on a *verde oliva scuro* (dark olive green) background. Finally, the S.79 has standard *grigio azzurro chiaro* (light blue-grey) undersides.

25
S.79 256-3 of 256ª *Squadriglia,* 108° *Gruppo,* 36° *Stormo Aerosiluranti,* Gerbini, Sicily, spring 1943

After completing night torpedo training, 36° *Stormo* resumed active service from 22 May 1943, flying mostly from the airfields at Milis, in Sardinia, and Gerbini, in Sicily. In June 1943 its 108° *Gruppo* joined the *Rgpt AS*, after which it gained autonomous status from 15 July 1943 following the disbandment of 36° *Stormo* and its twin unit, 109° *Gruppo*. This bomber features a white tail cross with the central Savoy crest, plus a white unit code and red individual numeral '3'. The fuselage band has been oversprayed in grey to reduce visibility, and the usual fasces inside a blue roundel are on the engine cowling. The roundels are black on a clear background above and below the wings. There is a uniform finish of *verde oliva scuro* (dark olive green) overall on the uppersurfaces and spinners, while the undersides are *grigio azzurro chiaro* (light blue-grey).

26
S.79bis of *Reparto Speciale Aerosiluranti,* Istres, southern France, June 1943

The S.79bis, also known as the S.79-III (*terza serie*), was an improved version of the *Sparviero* with more powerful Alfa Romeo 128 engines, flame-dampers on the gun barrels and no ventral gondola. This variant equipped the *Reparto Speciale Aerosiluranti,* a special unit formed for Operation *Scoglio* (Operation *Rock* – the attack on Gibraltar on the night of 19/20 June 1943). Markings include a white tail cross with a central Savoy crest and a fuselage band applied in *grigio azzurro chiaro* (light blue-grey) rather than white. The aircraft is devoid of unit codes, and the roundels above and below the wings are black on a clear background. There are no fasces roundels on the central engine cowling. The uppersurfaces and propeller hubs are *verde oliva scuro* (dark olive green) overall, while the undersides are *grigio azzurro chiaro* (light blue-grey).

27
S.79 204-7 of 204ª *Squadriglia,* 41° *Gruppo, Raggruppamento Aerosiluranti,* Apulia, summer 1943

204ª *Squadriglia* was one of four units that formed the *Raggruppamento Aerosiluranti* in early June 1943. The white tail cross apparently lacks the Savoy crest, while the fuselage unit codes are painted in *azzurro* (light blue) and the individual numeral is red. The white fuselage bands on the *Raggruppamento*'s trimotors were usually darkened to reduce their visibility, as in this case. To the same ends the wing roundels are black on a clear background above and below the wings. The uniform camouflage was *verde oliva scuro* (dark olive green) uppersurfaces overall and black spinners. The undersides were *grigio azzurro chiaro* (light blue-grey).

28
S.79 B1-5 of 1ª *Squadriglia, Gruppo* 'Buscaglia', *Aeronautica Repubblicana,* Gorizia, northern Italy, February 1944

This AR *Sparviero* displays, on both sides of the fuselage, the Italian national flag with a yellow border fringed on three sides only – the forward edge is plain. Unit codes are black and white, and the individual numeral is red, being repeated in white aft of the cowling of the centre engine. The wing national squares are black, and have twin black fasces on a clear background above and below the wings. The uniform camouflage finish is overall *verde oliva scuro* (dark olive green) on the uppersurfaces and *grigio azzurro chiaro* (light blue-grey) on the undersides. The central engine spinner is white, while the other two are black.

29
S.79bis B1-09 of 1ª *Squadriglia, Gruppo* 'Buscaglia', *Aeronautica Repubblicana*, Perugia-Sant'Egidio, central Italy, April 1944
This aircraft sports the camouflage adopted from April 1944 for night operations (the unit flew mainly at night). The aircraft is finished in *verde oliva scuro* (dark olive green) overall, with darkened markings and code numbers painted in *grigio azzurro chiaro* (light blue-grey). On 6 April 1944 S.79bis MM22285 B1-09, piloted by Tenente Francesco Pandolfo and Maresciallo Sesto Moschi, barely escaped the great *Sparvieri* slaughter over Valdarno by Thunderbolts of the USAAF's 57th FG. Nearly four months later both pilots were shot down aboard S.79 B1-00 over Otocac, Croatia, by Mustang IIIs of No 213 Sqn.

Tenente Pandolfo survived, but Maresciallo Moschi and the other crewmen were killed.

30
S.79bis F2-02 of 2ª *Squadriglia, Gruppo* 'Faggioni', *Aeronautica Nazionale Repubblicana*, Lonate Pozzolo, northern Italy, autumn 1944
As of 12 October 1944, after receiving word that the great ace Buscaglia had lost his life while serving with the Allies, 1° *Gruppo Aerosiluranti* was renamed 'Faggioni' and the unit changed its identifying fuselage letter from 'B' to 'F'. The markings on this aircraft include the Italian flag bordered by a yellow outline fringed on three sides only, both on the fuselage and fin. Unit and individual codes are painted in *grigio azzurro chiaro* (light blue-grey). The national squares on the wings are black, having black twin fasces on a clear background above and below the wings. The camouflage is uniform, being overall *verde oliva scuro* (dark olive green) on the uppersurfaces, propeller hubs and undersides.

UNIT BADGES

1

The 36° *Stormo* badge featured the motto *'Con l'ala tesa a gloria o morte'* ('With wing stretched to glory or death').

2

The 89° *Gruppo* badge featured a Sardinian peasant fishing for paper ships flying British flags. The unit motto, in Sardinian, read *'Donami tempus che ti stampu'* ('Give me time so that I can punch you').

3

41° *Gruppo* adopted a red devil emblem, which photo evidence proves was applied to the unit's S.84s.

4

41° *Gruppo* also had a version of its emblem where the devil was in black. Both versions featured the Latin motto *'Usque ad inferos'* ('Up to hell').

5

105° *Gruppo*'s *'Divieto di caccia'* ('Hunting is forbidden') emblem was worn on the tail of some of its S.79s in 1942-43. Note that the calibres of the aircraft's 7.7 mm and 12.7 mm SAFAT machine guns have been detailed in the sign's 'small print'.

6

The 108° *Gruppo* badge featured the motto *'Ocio che te sbuso!'* ('Beware I'm about to pierce you!') in northeastern Italian dialect. Photo evidence proves that this marking was applied to the unit's S.84s.

7

The 130° *Gruppo* badge featuring the Latin motto *'Virtute duce comite fortuna'* ('With virtue as a guide and fortune as a companion'). This insignia was created by Tenente Ferruccio Lo Prieno, who was killed in action on 2 December 1942.

8

This version of the 130° *Gruppo* emblem had the Italian motto *'Sotto a chi tocca'* ('Forward the next'). The colours of the pirate are partly conjectural here due to the primary reference source being a black and white photograph.

9

The 132° *Gruppo* badge featured the motto *'Col cuore e con l'arma oltre ogni meta'* ('With heart and weapon beyond any goal').

10

The 204ª *Squadriglia* badge consisted of a torpedo-armed swallow on a blue background.

11

278ª *Squadriglia*'s famous 'four cats' badge, which featured the Latin motto *'Pauci sed semper immites'* ('Few but always aggressive'). It was derived from *Reparto Speciale Aerosiluranti*'s initial S.79 torpedo-bomber operations in 1940 with just four qualified aircrew, which were dubbed the *'Quattro Gatti'* ('Four Cats' is Italian slang for very few people).

12

279ª *Squadriglia*'s menacing 'skull and torpedo-bones' badge.

INDEX

Note: locators in **bold** refer to illustrations, captions and plates.

aerial torpedo tests 6
Aeronautica Cobelligerante **62,** 63
Aeronautica Sardegna 54
affectiveness of the S.79 87
Aichner, Martino 50, **51,** 51–52, **52,** 60–61, 62, 68

air force strength 72, 77, 79, 84
aircraft: Bristol Beaufighter fighter plane (UK) 21, 25, 29, 30, 33, 46, 50, 52, 53, 57, 63, 69, 70, 73; Bristol Blenheim 1F fighter plane (RAF) 15, 16, 22, 24; Cant Z.1007 bomber plane (Italy) 20, **47,** 48, 73, 77; Fairey Fulmar fighter plane (RAF) 13, 14, 16, 17, 18, 20, 21, 24, 48; Fiat CR.42 fighter plane (Italy) 15, 47, 49; Fiat G.55

fighter plane (Italy) 86; Hawker Hurricane fighter plane (RAF) 19, 29, 30, 49, 54, 55, 62; Martin Baltimore bomber plane (UK) **62,** 63, **79;** P-47 Thunderbolt fighter-bomber plane (US) 81, 85, 86; Supermarine Spitfire fighter plane (UK) 46, 51, 55, 60, 61, 62, 64, 65–66, 68, 81
Alfa Romeo 128 engine 71, **71**

Allied invasion of Sicily 72
Angelucci, Silvio **56,** 56–57
ANR (Aeronautica Nazionale Repubblicana) 80, **80,** 87, **87**; 1° *Gruppo* 'Buscaglia'/'Faggioni' 80–82, **81, 83, 84,** 85, 86, 89; 1ª *Squadriglia* **43,** 80, 84; 2ª *Squadriglia* **43,** 80, 81, 84, 85; 3ª *Squadriglia* 80, 84
anti-torpedo net barrages 11
attack near Bizerte **64,** 64–66
attacks after Axis surrender in Tunisia 69–70
attacks on British warships 46–47, **48,** 48–63, **50, 51, 52, 54, 55,** 64–65, 73–76
attacks on naval convoys and merchant shipping 13, **13,** 15, 16, **17,** 17–18, 20–26, **21, 22, 23, 25,** 28, 29–46, **32, 47,** 47–48, **48,** 53, 63–64, **68,** 68–69, **69,** 76, **76,** 90

Bari harbour, raid on 84
Barioglio, Camillo 24, 25, 26, 47
Berka airfield, attack on 47
Bernardini, Orazio 13, 16, 19, 26
Bertuzzi, Imerio **69,** 82, 83, **84,** 86
Bougie Bay, attacks in 59–63, **62**
Buscaglia, Carlo Emanuele 6, **8,** 9, 11, 13, 14, 15, **15,** 18, 19, **19, 21,** 22, 25, **28, 32, 34, 35,** 50, 51, **51,** 59, 60–61, **62,** 62–63, **80,** 86

Cannaviello, Vittorio 14, 15, 18, 54, 56, **75,** 75–76
Caponetti, Angelo **4,** 13, **13,** 15, 32, 49
Cappa, Franco **17**
Caresio, Manlio 26, 32, 47, 49, 56, 65, 66
casualties and losses 13, 20–21, 28, 48, 53, 56, 68, 69, 81–82, 85, 86–87
Cimicchi, Giuseppe 15, **15, 25,** 25–26, 27, 29, 55, 59, 64, 65–66, 67, 71, 76, **76**
Cimolini, Oscar 16, **16**
Cipelletti, Giuseppe **25**
Cipriani, Roberto 20, 21, 24, 31, 32, 57
combat against former German allies after the September 1943 armistice 77–79
combat debut at Alexandria 7–9, **8**
conversion of *Gruppi* to transport role 79, **79**
Copello, Carlo **8,** 11
Cyprus and Tobruk supply routes, attacks on 19–26, **21, 22, 23, 24**

Dattrino, Alberto **41,** 70, 73, 78
Dequal, Vincenzo 7, **7,** 9, 11, **34**
Di Bella, Francesco 'Ciccio' 20, **20,** 24, 25, 31, 32, 54, 57, 59, 64, 67, **70,** 71, **72,** 72–73, 74–75, 78

Erasi, Massimiliano **4,** 9, **9,** 10, **11,** 11–12, 27, 59, 67, 73, 78, **78**

Faggioni, Carlo 15, **15,** 16, 18, 19, **19,** 25–26, 29, 50, 59, 71, 73, 76, 77, 80, **80,** 81, **81,** 82
first successes against the Royal Navy **9,** 9–10
Free French Special Air Service 47
freighters disguised as neutral ships 26

Gaeta, Nicola **19,** 82
Gavdos naval battles 14, 16
Gibraltar raids 70–71, **71,** 82–84, **84**
Grafometro ship-aiming device 12, **12**
Graziani, Generale Giulio Cesare 13, 22, 25–26, 29, **30,** 50, 51, 55, **55,** 59, 63, 64, 67, 68, **70,** 71, 78, **79**
Grossi, Georgio 12, 14, 20, 21, 24

ICAF (Italian Co-Belligerent Air Force) 11–12, **62,** 63, 78, 79, **79**
Ingrellini, Mario **48,** 48–49
insignia 9, **14, 44–45,** 65, **65,** 95

Italian declaration of war on Germany 79
Italians fighting with the Germans after the armistice **80,** 80–86, **81, 83, 84, 85**

lack of torpedo hits 33
Libyan operational tour 26–27, **27**

Magagnoli, Dante 25, **25,** 26, 57, 71, 82
Maiore, Scelto Francesco 60, **60,** 63
Malta-bound convoys, attacks on 46–48, **47,** 53
Mancini, Urbano 66, 67, 68, **68**
Marescalchi, Enrico 48, **48,** 58, 70, 73, 75, 77
Marini, Giulio 22, 23, 27, **27,** 28, 29, 30, 32, **70,** 71, 73
Marini, Marino 82–83, 84, 86
medals and decorations 11, 12, **14,** 17, **17,** 19, **19,** 20, 25–26, 28, **29,** 32, 46, 48, **48,** 49, 50, 52, **56,** 57, **62,** 63, 65, **68, 72,** 75, **75, 76,** 78, **78, 79, 80,** 82, 84, **84,** 91
Melley, Franco **4,** 7, 23, 24, 31, **38,** 46, 47, 49, 53, 59, 63, 64, **70,** 71
Mojoli, Amedeo 7, 12, 17, 20, 21, 22
Muti, Ettore 29, **29,** 30, 32

naming of aircraft 10
nicknames for *RA* units 6, 9
night attacks 67, 69–70, **71,** 72–74, **74**
Nuclei AS (Addestramento Aerosiluranti) **54**; 1° Nucleo AS 12, **35,** 64, 67, 72, 89; 2° Nucleo AS 12, **37,** 49, 54, 72, **75,** 89; 3° Nucleo AS 12, 49, 54, 55, 57, 59, 64, 72, 89

oath of loyalty to the RSI **81**
Operations (British): *Halberd* (September 1941) 24–25, **25;** *Harpoon* (June 1942) **48,** 53; *Husky* (July 1943) 72; *LB* (May 1942) 46; *Pedestal* (August 1942) **4,** 24, 53–57, **54, 55;** *Substance* (July 1941) **20,** 20–21, 24; *Tiger* (May 1942) 17; *Torch* (November 1942) 58–60, **59;** *Treacle* (August 1941) 22
Operations (Italian): *Scoglio* (June 1943) **70,** 70–71, **71**

Pandolfo, Francesco 72, 81, 83, 85, **85**
partisan attacks on *Gruppo* 'Faggioni' 86
patriotism and duty 48
Pfister, Carlo 55, **55,** 59, 61, 62, 67, 68, **68**
problems with level bombers 6
Pucci di Barsento, Emilio 32, 33, **33,** 40

RA (Regia Aeronautica) 87; 3rd *Squadra Aerea* 72, 73, 75, 77; 4th *Squadra Aerea* 72, 73, 74, 75; *Gruppo Aut AS:* 3° *Gruppo* 17; 24° *Gruppo* 47, 49; 34° *Gruppo* (281ª *Squadriglia*) 14, 15–16, 18, 20, **75,** 88; 67ª *Squadriglia* 13, 16; 68ª *Squadriglia* 14, 16, **20**; 41° *Gruppo* **33, 44,** 69, 73, 76, 78, 88, 95; 204ª Squadriglia 32, 33, **39, 42, 45,** 52, 53, **74,** 77, 78, 95; 205ª Squadriglia 29, **30,** 32, **32,** 33, **39, 40, 41,** 52, 69, 72, 77; 89° *Gruppo* **44,** 51, 68, 69, **69,** 95; 102° *Gruppo Tuffatori* 55; 104° *Gruppo* 47, **47,** 67, 69, 70, 72, 73; 252ª *Squadriglia* 49, 53, **53,** 77; 253ª *Squadriglia* **40, 41,** 48, **48,** 49, 53, **53,** 57, 73, 75, 77; 105° *Gruppo* **44,** 54, 58, 64, 67, 68, 95; 254ª *Squadriglia* 41, 56, 59, 63, 66; 255ª *Squadriglia* 53, 55, 56, **56,** 59, 63; 108° *Gruppo* **44,** 63–64, 69, 76, 95; 256ª *Squadriglia* **42,** 72; 109° *Gruppo* 47, 54, 72; 130° *Gruppo* **4,** 24, 26–27, **38, 45,** 47, 48, 56, 58, 65, **65,** 67, 72, 75, 95; 278ª *Squadriglia* 9–10, 11–12, **16,** 17, 21, 24, 25, 26, 31, **34, 35, 36,** 77, 88; 280ª *Squadriglia* 12, **17,** 17–18, 20, 21, **21,** 22, 23, 24, 26, 31, 32, 46, 49, 54,

56, 59, 63, 64, **65,** 66, 88; 281ª *Squadriglia* 12, 13, 14–15, **15, 16, 16,** 18, **18,** 19, **20, 21, 22, 22,** 23, 25, 26, **26,** 27, 27, 28, **28,** 29, 35, 88; 283ª *Squadriglia* 12, 20, 21, 23, 24, 26, **36, 37,** 46–47, 49, 53, 54, 59, 63, 64, 66, 88; 131° *Gruppo* 31, 69, 76, 88; 279ª *Squadriglia* 12, 13, **13,** 14, **14,** 15, 16, 18, 19, 22, 23, 26, 27, 28, 29, 30, **36, 37, 45,** 52, 69, 72, 88, 95; 284ª *Squadriglia* **9,** 12, 27, 29, 30, **38,** 47, 52, 69, 88; 132° *Gruppo* ('Buscaglia') **31, 40, 45,** 51, **51, 54, 55, 55,** 58, 59–60, 62, 63, 64, 66, 67, 68, **68, 69,** 72, 75, 76, **76,** 77, **78,** 79, **80,** 88–89, 95; 278ª *Squadriglia* **31,** 32, **38, 45,** 73, 77, 95; 281ª *Squadriglia (Stormo Baltimore)* **31,** 32, 78, **79**; 133° *Gruppo* 33–46, **39,** 89; *Gruppo Trasporti* 79; *Stormo AS:* 9° *Stormo* **47,** 48; 32° *Stormo AS* 59, 89; 36° *Stormo AS* 47, 53, 54, 59, 70, 89, 95 *see also ANR (Aeronautica Nazionale Repubblicana)*
RAF: NAS (Naval Air Squadron) 13, 17–18, 20, 21, 28, 47, 48, 49, 50, **50,** 53, 54, 55; No 43 Sqn 68, **68;** No 81 Sqn 51, 60, 66; No 242 Sqn **4,** 64, **65;** No 248 Sqn 53, 55
reconnaissance sorties 19, 33, 56, 59
reorganization of units 16, 18, 22, 27, 29, 31, 32, 33, 63, 77, 79, 80, 82, 86
Reparto Speciale Aerosiluranti 7, **8, 42,** 71–72, 87, 89
Repubblica Sociale Italiana 80, **81**
Rgpt AS (Raggruppamento Aerosiluranti) 69, 72, 73–74, **74,** 77
Rivoli, Ugo 21, **21, 26,** 31, 55, **55**
Robone, Guido **8,** 9, 16, 18, **34**
Rovelli, Luigi 22, 26, 27, **27,** 28
Royal Navy 23; HMS *Antelope* (destroyer) 49, 50; HMS *Argus* **4,** 46, 49, 50, **51, 69;** HMS *Ark Royal* (aircraft carrier) 17, 20, 24; HMS *Barham* (battleship) 25, **26,** 30; HMS *Bedouin* (destroyer) **51,** 51–52, **52;** HMS *Cairo* (cruiser) **4,** 53; HMS *Eagle* (aircraft carrier) 46, **48,** 48–49; HMS *Liverpool* (cruiser) 9, 10, **11,** 49–50; HMS *Queen Elizabeth* (battleship) 18, 25, **26**

Second Battle of Sirte, the **4,** 30–31
selection of ace pilots for Operation *Scoglio* **70,** 70–71
Setti, Alessandro 23, 25, 31, 49, 59
Silva, Lelio 25, 49–50, **50**
slaughter of Italian planes December 1942 64–66
Souda Bay, attack at 11
Sparviero S.79 6, **8,** 9, **9, 79, 87**; 205-6 **33, 40,** 93; 253-8 **40,** 93–94; 253-10 **41,** 53, 94; 254-1 **1,** 59, 66, 94;254-7 54, 59, 66; 278-1 9, 10, **34, 36, 40,** 92, 94; 278-3 16–17, **17, 35;** 280-1 **12,** 21, 49; 280-2 **4,** 17, 47, 49; 280-5 17, **17,** 21, 32, 49; 280-6 **4,** 21, **38,** 46, 53, 64, 93
Sparviero S.79bis (S.79-III) 43, 71, **71,** 72, 81, 82, 83, 84, **85,** 94
strike rates 12, 20, 28, 32, 87

'torpedo and skull' insignia **14**
torpedo-bomber role 6
torpedo load 7, **8**
torpedoes 7, 12, **61**
training 7, 12, 18, 67, 79, 80, 82, **87,** 89, 92, 94

Unia, Carlo 12, 67–68, 71, 72
use of *Sparvieri* after the war 79

Vellere, Antonio 59, 63, 64, **64,** 65

warship kills 90